Better
Every
Day

Also by Dorothy Wilhelm

No Assembly Required
The Pocket Book of Answers To Questions
You Never Got Around To Asking

Catch the Christmas Spirit
And Keep It All Year Long!

Better Every Day

By Dorothy Wilhelm

NTL Editions
Never Too Late For Joyful Living Series

Published in the United States of America by NTL Editions
Printed in the United States
Never Too Late
PO Box 881
DuPont, WA 98327

ISBN paperback: 978-0-692-32974-0

Cover Photograph by Canstock photo
Cover and typesetting by Sue Balcer, just your type.biz

First edition

Better Every Day Better Every Day 1. Joyful living 2. Laughter and health 3. Humor 4. Life change 5. Senior living 6. Health

Dedication

To Tai Chi Steve and the Inscrutable Gary for teaching this great-grandmother that if you keep moving, the years can't catch up to you.

To Li Huang because he doesn't mind getting up early on Saturday mornings and to Sally and Tammy. You know why.

To the new student in Tai Chi: Mary Jane, age 97

And as always, to my kids, grandkids, and great-grands. Without you life couldn't be better every day.

******

Author's note:

It has been suggested that in this book I have not portrayed my Tai Chi instructors as the wonderful, warm, caring people they are. That in fact, I've made them look strict and inflexible. I have just one thing to say. Nuh-Uh! What I showed were the worthwhile struggles everyone has to endure if they're to achieve results of value and I'm very proud of my results. Just for those who wonder, I started barely able to move my feet, and now, I really can get my knee up to hip level. Usually.

A Special Thanks

No book goes together without careful editing and since my own style of composition is decidedly free form, I need more editing than most so special thanks to my editors:

Gina (Eagle Eye) Wilhelm

Dr. Phil Venditti

and of course

Sally Everding

Contents

Foreword

My mother captured a porcupine the year before I was born, at the end of a long, raw Montana winter. The porcupine wandered onto our porch, and she threw a box over him. That's how she found out that just because you catch a porcupine, you don't necessarily have a porcupine. The whole town turned out to watch the drama as Mom tried to convince the porky that he should give up his prickly ways and become her pet. She was desperately lonely and just wanted something of her very own. The porcupine had a hard time seeing the advantage.

Seeing the proceedings had become dull, the Evans twins began to take turns lifting up the corner of the box, catching a squealing glance at the porky, and then dropping the corner among screams and giggles. My mother rounded on them, "Don't tease him! Don't tease the porcupine," she shrieked.

Well, the day wore on and though my mother lifted the box and pushed in leaves and twigs in the hope that the porcupine would find them a tasty snack, It was clear he wasn't coming out, and she sure wasn't getting in. Finally, as my mother wept, my father took charge. "Oh, Marion," my father said, "you know you can't keep this thing. You know you can't. Where would he stay? What would you feed him?" "Leaves and bark and things," my mother muttered sulkily. "I could keep it. I would train it," she insisted stubbornly. My father sighed. He reached over and tipped the box up, swatting after the porcupine with the broom as it scuttled away, and Mom cried. Dad shook his head. He adored his bride. Barely 17, she was a wild thing who couldn't cook, and wouldn't sew, but made the ramshackle cabin more livable with pictures cut from newspapers. She climbed the smokestack of the old mill because she was so bored. She wanted something of her own so badly. For me, that porcupine has always been a metaphor for all the sticky situations and prickly people we encounter every day. When porcupines are newborn they are tiny enough to fit two or three in the palm of the hand, soft and adorable they'll whimper for milk. But like us, they get old and crusty. They're not cute anymore and everybody stays away from them.

It seems to me that we're all porcupine trainers whether we want to be or not; tripping over porcupine people and situations that are unavoidable along the way.

As we enter our second 50 years, the tripping

seems to become more pronounced and the avoiding gets harder and harder. As soon as you pass that birthday in which the government takes undue interest, the daily mail begins to include stacks of brochures from people who seem to believe that the high point of life from now on is going to be choosing the perfect nursing home or cemetery plot. I was actually offered a contract for a TV commercial in which I would look earnestly into the camera and say, "I always wanted to be cremated." I just hoped they planned to wait til I was dead first.

Just the same, amazing and exciting things continue to happen. There's a new student in my Tai Chi class. She's 97 years old. We can keep growing, and life gets better every day. From the beginning, it's a question of adjusting and moving ahead.

In those cold Montana days, there was no electricity and there was no refrigeration except an occasional piece of ice cut from Flathead Lake in the winter. You could hang a few refrigerables high on the porch. No use storing up treasures on Earth, we already lived in paradise—with bears.

My parents saved up $35 for a doctor, and right after Christmas set off for Kalispell where I was born in a boarding house, delivered by Dr. Karns and his nurse, Mary Lou. My father said that as nearly as he could tell, I was the first baby any of the four of them had ever seen. Years later, speaking in Montana, I told about my birth and a gentleman in the audience stood up. "Dr. Karns delivered me, too," he said. "He's gotten lots better at it." Well good. That should be true. For all of us, it's got to get better every day.

Dorothy Wilhelm
June 20, 2015

A Note of Thanks

This is a collection of previously published newspaper columns.

Most of them appeared first in the Tacoma News Tribune.

When I first started to write for the Dear Old Trib, my editor was Gary Jasinek. He said, "Everyone knows you're where it's at for people over 50 in the Puget Sound area." Twenty-five years and many editors have helped me since then, and I still don't know what the heck he meant. But I am and have always been grateful for the wonderful support of The News Tribune staff. I hope it will always feel like home.

What Goes Around

I hadn't ridden a Ferris wheel for years, but I always thought they were the most romantic conveyances on earth. You know, snuggling in a rickety little car with the wind streaming past your ears, rocketing through the air with screams all around. Good stuff. Now that I've come to the place where my morning e-mail features banner headlines promising to "Lower Your Burial Insurance," I feel entitled to cling to a few fantasies. Never mind, the dream is over.

Last weekend I rode on the Great Wheel in Seattle and to tell the truth, I thought it was lame. It's all enclosed glass cars, no more exciting than a tearoom. There's no wind in your hair, no mindless screams, no risk to life or limb. What kind of fun is that? Worse yet, I realized that even if I could find someone to share a romantic adventure, nothing about me scrunches up enough to make thrill-ride romance practical anymore.

When one dream dies, you must find another, and in this beautiful summer it was easy to find. My grandson, 13, traveling alone for the first time, came from Minnesota to visit. His father, a Super Fan of Northwest sports, asks that we call the boy "Ichiro," or simply "Junior." I mostly call him "Honey." We got reacquainted. I adjusted to his new deep voice and the fact that he's a vegetarian now. We enjoyed all the touristy things. We rode the Ducks in Seattle, saw the sharks at Point Defiance, and spent a cold, snowy, wonderful day on Mt. Rainier. And of course we rode the Great Wheel.

There were exciting excursions with uncles, aunts and cousins. "Honey" is lucky to live near his maternal grandparents so he knows them well, and his mother has done a great deal of family history research. When I started to tell him about my own family and my father's parents I realized that I don't know much about them for sure.

Researching family history has never been more popular than it is today, due to easy internet access to records, but I needed more personal help. I found it at the Heritage Quest Research Library in Sumner, WA, where volunteers assist 2000 visitors a year in finding free, hands-on help with family research.

Soon I had results in hand and I could tell "Ichiro" that my father's family left the poverty of Ireland for the Virginia Colony before the American War for

Independence. I've had ancestors in every war from the Revolution on. Apparently we couldn't get along with anybody.

Over an all-vegetarian taco dinner, I told my grandson about the family I do remember. I told him about him about my mom, who died on the fifth of July, nearly two decades ago, long before he was born. I always thought she stayed with us through the Fourth, because she just couldn't stand to leave before the party was over.

My mother loved celebrations. When she gave a party—and she was always giving a party—she invited everyone from the fellow at the gas station to Mr. Morietti down the block who mended shoes. The guest list included clergy and the homeless. She believed in people and they almost never disappointed her. *Psychology Today* reports a study showing that people who deceive themselves into thinking the world is a wonderful place are much happier than those who are more realistic and see the world as it really is. For Mom, the world was always in danger of breaking out into joy. She had been dirt poor growing up, lived in a tarpaper shack in the early days of her marriage—and was the richest woman I ever knew. However, she was no pushover. One day she found a stranger inside her car. He had broken in and was rummaging in the glove compartment. She chased him through six blocks of Spokane's back alleys. She then threw her five-foot frame against him in a flying tackle and sat on him nonchalantly until the police arrived.

My mother had no time for negative people; "Flush him down the toilet!" was her standard dismissal. For a girl who lived much of her life with no indoor plumbing, that seemed an elegant solution to any vexing problem.

In years to come, my young visitor and I will look back at our summer and remember the exciting things we did, but I'll know it was the shared time that mattered. It's up to us to keep the celebration going.

After my grandson returned home, he sent me roses.

July 1, 2014

Smile, Darn Ya, Smile

My Number Two son was 14 years old when he experienced an epic growth spurt. (My children insist that their names not appear in print, so I am reduced to calling them by number or other creative designations. When you know my son better, you may want to call him by the more familiar Two.) Anyway, in just a few months, Two shot up more than eight inches, and almost overnight he was well over six feet tall. He found it difficult to get used to his new size. He spilled things, knocked chairs over, fell through stationary objects and caused furniture to crash to the floor, often in surrounding homes.

Naturally, I offered support and encouragement. "Will you watch what you're doing?" I'd helpfully scream. He spilled; I yelled. One day he suddenly turned on me and demanded, "How can you keep yelling at me? Can't you see that my arms don't even end in the same place they did yesterday?"

I feel the same way about these second 50 years of life. It's like a protracted adolescence. No part of my body ends where it used to or does what it used to do. There is no owners' manual, and everybody else says they know what will be best for me far better than I do.

At Tai Chi this morning, our instructor, Tai Chi Steve (I suspect that's not his real name) had the temerity to command us to raise our knees to the level of our hips. Think now. What are the chances? Most of us don't even have our original hips and knees. Some students could actually do it. I may never forgive them.

For some reason, my children seem to think this is a good time to bring up stories from their past that can't be substantiated. For instance, there's a rumor around that I used to keep a big wooden spoon hanging in the kitchen to smack kids who misbehaved, gently and lovingly, of course. A perfect example of imperfect memory—theirs, not mine. That spoon was strictly for stirring spaghetti sauce. Mostly.

Somehow, when the kids were younger it was easier to feel in control. The other day at the Y, I saw a mother lead her two small children—about three and five—into an unoccupied handball court. She shut the door and sat down happily outside with a book while the children ran, yelled and literally bounced off walls. She could see them. They really couldn't get hurt—and better yet, they couldn't get out. I don't think you can reserve the court for that purpose, but for about minutes, that mom looked very happy. Finding our bliss is up to us.

International speaker and humorist Dr. Patt Schwab of Seattle says a lasting feeling of joy can start with a simple smile. Dr. Schwab notes that an important step is reaching out to others. "Make a promise to yourself to make five people smile today," she says, "because when they smile, you'll smile." If five smiles are too many to try for, start with three. If you're just too shy to reach out to someone else, make yourself smile five times in the day. Start by smiling at yourself in the mirror. Do it first thing in the morning before you dress and you'll probably laugh out loud.

Patt Schwab creates her own brand of joy and bemusement by carrying a regiment of rubber chickens around with her. They range from miniature key ring size to full size—undressed for success—creatures. Why rubber chickens? She swears they are the antidotes for any "fowl mood." It's hard to assess what is so endearing about rubber chickens, but Dr. Schwab regularly shares her fowl humor with international audiences who love her and clamor to take a chicken home (http://www.fundamentallyspeaking.com).

Number Two son eventually stopped growing. He folded his tall frame happily into a Navy jet and flew off for 20 years or so. His elder brother looked after him thoughtfully and remarked, "You know, Mom, if you had hit him over the head with that wooden spoon as often as you did me, he'd be a lot shorter and a lot nicer."

You see there's another gross exaggeration. Would I hit them with the same spoon I stirred dinner with? That would not be sanitary. Besides, height is in the genes. It does make me smile to remember, though. Now, I only need four more smiles for today.

March 1, 2015

Who You Calling Sheveled?

On his last visit to my little condo here in Pleasantville, Number One son walked around my kitchen closing cupboard doors for about an hour. I actually don't see any great point in cupboard doors being closed. You can't see what's inside. It's like making beds or paying taxes. You'll just have to open them up again.

When every door was tightly closed, he sat down with me, patted my hand, and said in a very kind and gentle voice, "Now, Mother, we (I think he means his five siblings) have been talking and we wish you would try to do little things like close the cupboard doors and not pile your dirty dishes in the sink for more than three or five days and remember not to put them in the cupboard until they're washed. Because it all makes you look so disheveled.

"And Mother, we just wish you would try to be just a little more"—he searched for the right word —, and found it. "Sheveled! We wish you could be more sheveled."

No use being offended. He's right. I'm not sheveled. In fact, we're talking about a club in which I have no hope of being considered for membership.

One dictionary source says that words like "sheveled" are lost positives. They are words that probably once had a positive prefix but they're gone now. I can relate to that, because I'm always losing things, too.

You can always recognize sheveled people. Their makeup is smooth and uncaked. Their mascara never runs. They walk easily in high heels. Even the guys. And they cook meals from gourmet magazines.

My kids are much neater and far more organized than I. They all married people so organized that they make Martha Stewart look haphazard and slovenly. I can't imagine how it happened. Some recessive gene won the battle for survival, I guess, but it's given me a terrible inferiority complex.

Disheveled people, on the other hand, struggle to find socks that match because either the washing machine or the dog ate several. They prepare meals from whatever two or three ingredients are on hand and are likely to find the cat on the table sometime during the meal. This is especially troublesome if they don't own a cat. Our local newspaper, which I read daily (I am disheveled but loyal) is very sheveled. Recently it printed easy directions for making slipcovers by just sewing one seam. I cut them out and imagined myself creating a whole new look for my living room, but in the end I made a slip cover for my office chair just by stuffing foam cushions into pillowslips. No sewing. You just sit down really, really fast, holding the cushions in place with a series of skillful motions of your gluteal muscles. You get aerobic exercise along with your new slipcovers. What could be better?

I spent 50 years teaching my kids to be true to themselves. It may be time to take my own advice. If you have friends and keep them, if you have goals and enjoy pursuing them, if you enjoy one sunrise and one sunset each day, maybe it doesn't matter whether you're sheveled or not. That's such a good thought; it's enough to make me feel positively gruntled.

June 4, 2008

Can You Believe We Did That?

The first bottle of root beer exploded at just about 10 o'clock in the morning on the Fourth of July. As usual. We need those time-honored traditions to get a holiday off to the right start. Our tradition was that my mother always made root beer for the Fourth of July and it always exploded before anyone could drink it. I won't say that Independence Day was better when I was a child, but it certainly was more interesting.

Soft drinks didn't come in cans in those days. If you wanted root beer, you had to go to a soda fountain in some big town like Libby or you had to make it yourself. We'd all seen pictures of Santa Claus holding a bottle of his preferred soft drink, but he'd certainly never brought any to Warland, Montana. It was pretty generally agreed that a proper Independence Day celebration required root beer, and Old Man Dean—as far as I know, his mother named him "Old Man," for he was always called by that name— did the honors for many un-eventful years, until the game warden invited him to the Lincoln County seat for an extended stay. My mother volunteered bravely to take over the chore. I have no idea why. The first year her brew was perfect. That really was unfortunate, because that convinced Mother that she was a gifted brewer of root beer, and every year after that she made it, and every year it exploded.

Root beer really shouldn't be that hard to brew, at least theoretically. Flavoring, sugar and water are all you need, according to www.hoptech.com. The problem is the fizziness. If you don't put in enough ale yeast, the drink is flat; too much, and you have shrapnel flying all over the yard.

After the explosions stopped and the glass was raked to the side of the yard for another year, we all walked down the road to taste Betty Evans' new batch of traditional Fourth of July pickles. They were just terrible as always, tasting strongly of kerosene. "Don't you say anything bad about Mrs. Evans' pickles," hissed my mother, putting her patented pinch/grab hold on my shoulder. "It's an old family recipe," Betty Evans said with satisfaction. Apparently it was acquired from a family member who was not wholly friendly. I really could have used the root beer to wash it down.

We had no way of knowing that would be our last

Fourth of July there by the Kootenai River. World War II started that winter and the whole town moved to Spokane for defense work. Santa started taking his bottled soft drinks to the troops overseas, and then after that he was busy trying to teach the world to sing in perfect harmony. Now that I'm grown up, of course, I endorse the idea of Safe and Sane celebrations. Looking back, though, it seems that always, in those years and after, our best celebrations were those tinged with humor and maybe a bit of danger where you shake your head and say, "Can you BELIEVE we did that?"

For instance, when the Coast Guard Barque Eagle visited our town for the Tall Ships celebration, I couldn't help remembering another Fourth of July when my son sailed on Eagle. I dampened his celebration considerably by actually calling the admiral to complain that my son wasn't writing to me often enough. Can you BELIEVE I did that? He sure started writing though. I don't believe I'd do that again.

A close friend, celebrating her recovery from heart surgery as she rounds the corner toward 80, treated herself to the girls' Schwinn bike she never had as a child. "I can't BELIEVE you did that," I said. "It sure is fun," she says, as she rides around the neighborhood. Also, she reflects, it's much more comfortable than the boy's bike she used to own. Yes, she has a safety helmet. Our celebrations don't have to be wrapped in plastic and they should reflect who we are right now.

Here in Pleasantville we had our usual picture-perfect Fourth of July. The food was perfect, the pickles were crisp without a hint of kerosene and nothing exploded. Nothing at all. I can't believe we did that. I think I'll just look around and see if I can't find that old root beer recipe.

July 1, 2009

Memory of My Home Town

The plain manila envelope came with Friday's mail. It contained a slender magazine called *The Trail*, published by Lost Trail Publishing in Trego, Montana. On the first page was an ad for a funeral home in Libby and a casino at Roosville Crossing, but it was the second page that made me stop to catch my breath. It was a full-page photograph of Warland, the tiny Montana town where I spent my first eight years of life. It may be hard to believe now when pictures from all around the world land in our e-mail inboxes every few minutes, but I had never seen a picture of that little town, even when I lived there. From my growing-up years, there are only a few black and white snapshots of neighbors and family stuffed in an anonymous cardboard box in the garage. Cameras able to take landscape pictures were rare.

Warland, Montana, established in 1904 by the Great Northern Railroad, doesn't exist anymore. It lived only 68 years and was obliterated when Libby Dam created the 370-foot-deep Lake KooCanUsa from the waters of the Kootenai River. My home is somewhere under the water. It is unsettling to have outlived the years of my hometown.

"We don't know," read the caption under the black and white picture, sent by Publisher Gary Montgomery, who knows my roots, "about the identity of these ramshackle buildings in the foreground." Well, let me tell you. Those ramshackle buildings were the homes of railroad section gang workers like my father. They were little more than tarpaper shacks, raked by wind and cold and dust. Mother tried to make our home a little prettier and a little more resistant to the blast of winter winds with the addition of scraps of newspaper applied to the walls with flour and water paste.

There was no electricity or plumbing. Our water source was a pipe that came out of the ground across the road from our house, and in the spring the water had plump green worms in it. Protein is always welcome.

The picture shows the sawmill where a fire spelled the end of lumbering in Warland. Children were told the Old Mill was haunted, which made it irresistible. There's the general store and the stationmaster's office, which had the town's only phone. There's the ferry, which was the only way to cross the great Kootenai River until the Civilian Conservation

Corps built a bridge in the late '30s. The CCC was made up of unmarried men, so my joyously single Aunt Vi, a professional wrestler, came to live with us and promptly became engaged to two-thirds of the bridge builders. I don't know how the other third got away. She was soon planning rather a large wedding. It never actually took place, and I was sort of sorry.

I remember weeping as I walked up and down between the rows of potato plants doing the hated job of looking for potato bugs to drop to their doom in a can of kerosene, a perfectly acceptable chore for a five-year-old. I remember the terrible sledding accident on the hill by the one-room schoolhouse schoolhouse after the train had gone for the day so help couldn't be called. I went roller-skating on Mondays in that white building, which was a dance hall on Saturday night and a church on Sunday morning, if the minister remembered to come.

It never occurred to us in those days, when we stood with patient fixed smiles waiting for the click of someone's Kodak Brownie camera, that one day we might have cameras that would take gorgeous pictures, which would instantly be seen around the world. But now, lost in computer Hades, they're just as inaccessible as those boxes in my garage.

It's true that we are what we were—but we also are who we think we were. When you're lucky enough to find something to validate your remembered past you can pull it around you like an old but comfortable coat. If you bring those bits and pieces of memory out to share, you'll certainly find that they still have a lot of warmth and wear left in them.

July 30, 2013

Are You My Buddy?

I was five years old on the spring morning when my mother and I flagged the early train in Warland, Montana, for our trip to the hospital in Libby. I'd never seen a hospital before and I was not impressed.

After I struggled into a flannel nightie, the nurse asked if I would like to ride a pony. Now, I happen to have a particular fondness for ponies, so naturally I said yes. I'm not ashamed to admit it. I trustingly put my hand in hers and the next thing I knew, I was lying in a bed with a very sore throat, which, I was told, was because my tonsils were gone. I didn't know what tonsils were, so that didn't bother me too much. I had lots of ice cream, but I never laid eyes on that pony and I'm still plenty annoyed about that.

Luckily this potentially traumatic experience left no permanent scars other than a certain skepticism about combining ponies and hospitals. Still, I have to admit that I got in touch with some very deep-seated anxieties when I checked into the hospital for surgery this spring and then suddenly found myself scheduled for a repeat of the same surgery only three months later. It was completely incomprehensible. I hadn't even mentioned ponies to anyone.

While I recovered from the first surgery, my six children took the maximum leave time they had available to come home and be with me. It was practically worth learning to do without a few assorted spare parts, just to spend that quality time with them. When time came for the unexpected second surgery, though, all of my support people had already used their available time. I felt more than a bit panicky. I was going to need help, and I had no idea where it might come from. How could I manage?

I calmly reverted to my customary thinking mode, which involves cuddling into an old flannel bathrobe, warmed in the dryer, while I skillfully carved the centers from a two-pound box of soft chocolates with a teeny tiny spoon. In the time it took me to eat a single layer of soft centers, I had the solution in my hand. I didn't think of it myself, of course. It was handed to me by Daughter #1, who organizes us through all our catastrophes. I don't know how she does it. She didn't even get any chocolate.

"Your task is simple," she told me. It always makes me nervous when a sentence starts that way. "You just have to call 10 friends who will agree to be your support person for each of the first 10 days you're alone after surgery." "That will never work," I said. That week the papers were full of the Duke University study about relationships among Americans, which showed that most of us don't have one good friend— let alone 10. "We'll call it your Buddy List," she went on, as if I had not spoken. "Each person will know they're on call for just one day. They'll be available for whatever is needed—maybe to give you a ride to the doctor's office, pick up groceries or prescriptions or perhaps give nothing but a little encouragement."

"Why on earth will they do that?" I asked.

"Because people want to help," she said firmly, "and the best part is that each person knows in advance the day they'll be needed so it does away with the lame, 'Call me if you need something.'"

So began the cycle of phone calls that started with a rather plaintive, "Are you my buddy?" Did it work? Yes. So well that I actually had requests for a second day. One friend wrote me a letter thanking me for the gift of MY time!!

It turns out my daughter was right. People really do want to help. "The hardest thing, Mom," my son said on his day with me, "is that sometimes we have to ask for what we need."

One day soon, I'll be called upon to be on a friend's

buddy list. At least I hope so, because like everyone else, I want to help. But if they as much as mention ponies, I'm out of there.

February 13, 2007

The Cane Mutiny

It was just mid-morning when they passed the joint around. I had never held one in my hands before, and it was much heavier than I expected. "Now that," the class leader caroled happily, "is the part the doctor may be using for those of you who are having the hip replacement surgery." I squinted suspiciously at the heavy metal object in my hand. It looked like a trailer hitch with a fancy knifelike curved stem. She continued with determined cheerfulness, "The doctor will just cut off the top of your thigh bone—it's called the femur—and pound this one in place." He'll do what? This was an image I just wasn't enjoying. I began to calculate the number of steps it would take for me to get to the door and out of it, using my purple cane with the orange sunbursts. I imagined myself raising my hand and saying, "I just remembered there's something in the car I have to get (I have to get the heck out of here)." But I stayed and I'll be starting this New Year with a completely new replacement for my otherwise sagging anatomy.

At the joint class, we were each supplied with a spiral-bound Hip (or Knee) Replacement Manual just packed with helpful tips and ideas. "Plan meals ahead," it says. "Cook individual meals and freeze them." Now, where is the fallacy there? When did I last cook anything? I looked in the freezer thinking I must have some dishes on hand. And sure enough, there were a number of dishes in there. They all seemed to be empty. I suppose I was saving them to wash at a more convenient time.

But, I am freezing things. So far, I've frozen a bag of almonds and a pair of nylons. It's supposed to prolong their life, and that way, I can assure my daughter the nurse that yes, of course, I have a variety of things in the freezer. We're making changes. My son the engineer installed grab bars and took out the glass shower doors in the bathroom. My ace in the hole is Diane Malone, whose business offers supplementary services from cooking and driving to changing dressings for folks recovering from surgery or otherwise needing aid. If you're lucky, there's someone like Diane in your community. Look under Elder Care Management in the yellow pages.

The manual gives projected times for resuming day-to-day activities: Eight to twelve weeks for driving, six weeks to return to work part-time, resume sexual activity in four to six weeks. Since this was last an issue just after the Pleistocene era, that's a surprise. But my doctor did say I'd be astounded at the change in my quality of life. If that does happen, I will certainly call for new underwear. There's actually a website where you can assist in a virtual hip replacement surgery online. You are guided by an animated "Dr. Fisher" through the whole surgery, from scrubbing your hands to sending the patient to recovery. "Way to slice," enthuses the doctor as you wield your scalpel. You actually tap the joint replacement in place. Tap. Tap.

Between the weather and my upcoming life lesson, I wasn't able to do any holiday traveling this year, but Grandson Matty, age 3, has concluded that I actually am waiting at the airport in Minneapolis if his parents would just go look. His Dad writes, "It's hard to tell where exactly Matt thinks you live. He has narrowed it down to the Humphrey Terminal (at Minneapolis-St. Paul Airport) or any airplane flying overhead. One thing is for sure: He thinks you own every airplane in the sky. Anyway, it annoys him that since the airport is so close by, we don't go see you more often." Me too.

I can't say I'm looking forward to the surgery. But I'm looking forward to discarding my cane and walking easily again. The minute it happens, you'll find me at the airport, because, you see, there's a young man waiting for me at the Humphrey Terminal in Minneapolis and I need to get there as soon as I can.

December 31, 2008

Hip Shot

See Dorothy. Dorothy has a brand new metal hip joint. It will cause disruption in airport security lines all over the world. See Dorothy walk.

"Sit like your mother told you NOT to sit. Sleep with a pillow between the knees," went the advice I received from Liz Lassoie, along with dozens of others from *News Tribune* readers. Liz exhorted me to keep the knees apart and never cross them, which certainly goes against the advice my daddy gave me. "Just do it like a man," was the advice an orthopedic surgeon gave her on how to manage dressing tasks like putting on socks and shoes. Liz wrote that she has had five joint replacement procedures and still managed to take up inline skating on Ruston Way.

But times have changed, and with new procedures nobody cares where you put your knees or how you sleep, at least after some hip replacement surgeries. That's not what my daddy told me, either, but I've found, to my delight, that new anterior hip replacement is very different than in the old posterior-approach days (as the original hip replacement surgery was described). Patients who experienced that approach are likely to feel like kids who went to camp before the good old days when they put in all the cool equipment. Today's class attends joint camp, complete with t-shirt, gourmet meal with spouse (though you did have to provide your own spouse) and even a flower from the doctor. My friend Rodney mourned his surgery several years ago: "I never got to even see a joint, let alone hold it, and they didn't even give me a t-shirt. All I got was this freakin' big scar." Recovery, we were told, would take less than a month, and there would be no limitations to physical activities. Hip replacement, an operation that about 300,000 Americans undergo each year, has been called one of the greatest aids in giving back normal life. It's sure been that for me.

My children came to spend time with me during surgery and recovery, arriving and departing on a fearsomely complicated roster created by my first born, the health-care professional. "It looks to me," said Number One son, "as if you planned this whole thing just to spend more time with your kids." Not true. But if I'd known it would work, I certainly would have done it sooner.

I learned to put on socks and dress with the items in my hip replacement kit, but I still needed help. The kids kept a journal of my general shortcomings.

There's an entry in the hand of my son, the Latin teacher. He brought a huge bag of tests to be graded while he watched over me. He had some trouble getting the bag through security but he got them all carefully graded. There's another in the careful but inscrutable side notes of my daughter, the actor. "Tylenol, stage right," she wrote.

"Mom is not enthusiastic about exercise. We'll have to work on that," notes an early journal entry. I didn't think I had to be enthusiastic. I thought I just had to do it. We were doing fine until yesterday, when Number Two son arrived for the final watch. He carries a sea bag and the ring tone on his cell phone is "A Pirate's Life For Me." Now he's just coming back from "a short little four-mile jog." He pores over the journal pages with what can only be described as fiendish delight.

"Make no mistake," he chortles, "you are in the hands of the only one of your children who will badger you unmercifully 'til you meet your rehab goals."

The last journal entry begins darkly, "In which we learn that we did NOT do our exercises yesterday." "Mom," he calls. "Have you done your exercises, Mom? It's time to walk! How about your cranberry juice?"

No precautions; no restrictions. No limitations.
See Dorothy run.

January 29, 2009

What, Me Worry?

"Most of what you worry about never really happens." My father was an ardent believer in that frequently repeated quote, but he took it one step further. If most of the things we worry about never happen, he reasoned, this must mean that only the things you don't worry about actually occur. Makes sense so far, but he went on: This makes it essential to worry about absolutely everything. If you omit any possible worry, that's the one thing that will invariably go wrong. It isn't easy to worry about everything, no matter how skilled a worrier you are. It's a heavy responsibility, and you need to involve as many co-worriers as possible. Dad's worry extended even to my mother's rolls baking on a Saturday morning. "You know, it doesn't seem as if they are browning the way they should," he'd fret. His record was very good. Hardly anything he worried about happened, and the rolls were always delicious. So I adopted his philosophy for my own and became a skilled, you might even say professional-level, worrier.

Because of this, I freely admit that I take full responsibility for the Seahawks' loss in a recent big football game (Super Bowl XLIX). Now, it may be that football is not a big part of your life. It may even be that you're one of those people who think the Sea Hawk is a mythical bird who never really got off the ground. Speaking of mythical, perhaps you're one of those sober and serious people who has never mashed a single avocado to make dip for your tailgate party. This means you have not worried about the Seahawks, so in a sense, the fact that they did not become the Super Bowl Champions is your fault, and Tom Brady had nothing to do with it.

I don't wish to pile guilt upon you, of course. I'm sure you may have had good reasons for not worrying, but still, facts are facts. I know that many books have been written about the uselessness of worry, but the facts are there. When I worry, the Seahawks win. When I don't, they lose (I wish to note that worry in no way takes the place of prayer. They're two different things, usually but not always involving different groups of people).

The holidays are past and the decorations removed, so that frees up a lot of time for recreational worry. Income tax, for instance: How will I pay? The geriatric head gasket on my car: How long will it last?

Trip to visit grandchildren: Must I fly?

It's a little known fact, I believe, that today's fine air safety record is entirely attributable to people like me who sit white-knuckled through every flight, worrying every minute. "Will we crash?" "Should the engine be making that noise?" "Do the flight attendants look nervous?" And it works. Air travel has never been safer.

Then there was Valentine's Day. Obviously I don't worry nearly enough about Valentine's Day. As far as I'm concerned, Cupid should tuck his plump little parts into his clothes, get dressed and go home. I did worry that I was not going to get any valentines and I got two—three, if you count the one from the cremation service. I didn't get any of the sort I used to love when the kids pasted little candy conversation hearts around a cardboard square to make a picture frame valentine for Mom. Those conversation hearts have been around since the Civil War. They have a shelf life of five years. At least. New phrases are added every year. Last year's new additions included "Table 4 Two," and "Top Chef." I certainly worry about that.

According to the National Retail Federation, two-thirds of men who purchased flowers for Valentine's Day sent them to their significant other, and a third of men sent flowers to their mothers. So if my math is right, 1¼ of my sons was planning to send me flowers. Statistically, this indicates that I should worry about the other ¾ of my offspring. But I didn't get any flowers at all, so now my worry includes 100% of the extended family.

I never worried about worrying. Everyone needs a hobby and I've been pleased by the results. Nobody believes you if you say everything will be okay, but it's easy to find people to share and expand upon your worries, especially on Fox News. According to *AgingCare.com*, excessive worrying can be responsible for a long list of severe health problems, including weakening of the immune system, panic attacks, irritable bowel syndrome and much, much more.

So I'm going to learn to worry less, starting very soon. I've already taken worry to the highest level. I worried about the Seahawks. I worried about Marshawn and I worried about Richard. To tell the truth, I never worried at all about Russell or Pete, but I worried about defense and I worried about turnovers.

But clearly either you or I didn't worry enough. That really worries me.

February 1, 2015

The Frog Who Came In From The Cold

I'm not not crazy about the tree frog in my coffee cup. I'm just glad I hadn't poured the coffee yet. It has slowed my caffeine intake way down. You see, I started the day as usual, bringing in the paper to read with that first cup of coffee, when—plop! this bright green little fellow dropped out of the rolled paper into my cup. Sort of a trojan newspaper, you could say.

It turns out that while there are tree frogs on every continent, there's only one species of tree frog in the Northwest, and for some reason they're holding a convention on my front porch. I must admit that this fact was of only passing interest to me—until a couple of weeks ago, when a small Pacific tree frog troupe began plotting a way to move into my house for the winter. Naturally, I'm sympathetic; after all, I've recently gone through the trauma of being forced to move, and I can see how a nice warm place to stay would be very attractive.

So now every morning at 6:30 a.m. I edge the screen door open, just a quarter of an inch at the time, with my frog fighting gear in hand. No sign of an intruder, but I have my weapon ready just in case. It's a four-inch plastic pot and a piece of thin flexible cardboard. What else would you use on a frog? They're cute and fashionable, being bright lime green in color—and we all know green is the new black, so he would accessorize the house nicely.

But I'm terrified that I'd step on him.

It's so traumatic I may never vacuum again. I'm glad to have the excuse.

Many of my friends suggested that I might bring PacFroggie inside and put him in a terrarium. I checked with Marc Hayes at the venerable Burke Museum in Seattle. "People who try to make pets of tree frogs usually don't keep them very long," Marc Hayes observes. They'll only eat live bugs—so you have to get them live fruit flies, and then you have to encourage the fruit flies to go in and get eaten, so it can get to be very time consuming.

I'd avoid it for another reason. Many years ago, when we were stationed at White Sands Missile Range, My husband caught a Horned Toad. He thought caring for this New Mexico denizen would be a good experience for the children. So they all spent the next three days in the desert heat digging up ants for the horned toad to eat. Then, they decided he would be happier in the desert, and we certainly were. So I'm not anxious to repeat that experience. I won't be capturing any of my little friends.

These frogs don't hibernate. Marc Hayes quotes the wisdom of the First Nation people of Canada. They believe that the frog embodies lessons of the past and hope for the future. That seems a lot to expect of a little creature barely an inch long, but Marc says what people desperately need today is hope for the future in the context of the avalanche of problematic environmental issues. The sensitivity of frogs, he feels, should allow us a way to develop hope for a good future. The greatest challenges of today, Marc continues, is climate change, because if we can limit climate change in a manner that keeps amphibians successful, we will likely maintain a better world for ourselves

So, ok, the frog stays maybe I just won't go out the front door. And you know, I was thinking the other day as I looked around at all of these bright green frogs, clinging to the doorframe and hopping over the welcome mat. There's got to be a prince in there somewhere.

I'll just think of this as an opportunity.

September 4, 2005

To Remove A Flat Frog

It took me a while to realize that the brown spot on my carpet was actually a small, flat frog. Naturally, I wasn't wearing my glasses at two o'clock in the morning and it wasn't moving around much, so I mistook the small creature for a spot; gravy perhaps, or maybe coffee. Here on the edge of a designated wetland, we have frog plagues of biblical proportions at least monthly, but usually the critters are bright green, small and lively. I didn't want to give too much thought to how this frog happened to be brown, small and flat—and in the middle of my carpet. He didn't seem to be dead, exactly, but he certainly wasn't too lively, either. Still, I feared that, startled into action, he might launch himself under the furniture and I'd never be able to evict him.

I will tell you right now that there are very few sources to give you advice on what to do with a flat frog at 2:00 in the morning. Get out any housekeeping book you want. How many tips for removing a frog do you find? Zero, that's how many. Although I did find directions for building a frog sanctuary using carpet strips. I pondered strategies for froggie resuscitation and even issued myself a deadline. If my unexpected guest hadn't moved by 2:30 a.m., I would declare it officially in a state of demise and conduct a ceremonial flushing.

"Why didn't you just pick it up and throw it out?" asked my son when I relayed my adventure. That's a very good question. To tell the truth, it would have been very different if this had happened during the day. I could have gone out and called a neighbor. "You won't believe what got into my house," I'd say. "Come on down for tea and help me resettle my frog." My upstairs neighbor is an Army Ranger. I'm sure I could call on him. But at night, questions of life and death loom large and insoluble and you really can't make any phone calls. I thought briefly of putting the critter in a box with air holes and overnighting it to my grandson who, at six, has a very scientific turn of mind. He would be delighted and he'd know just what to do with it.

Condo living does call for adjustments from both frog and human residents. The siding is being removed and replaced on our pocket paradise. We were instructed to move our plants inside while the work was done. I suppose this frog came in with one of the big plants, got up and wandered around in the night looking for a drink of water, and just flattened out. I'm just sure I didn't step on him. Probably.

Finally, it was time for action, so holding my breath, I dropped a white paper napkin shroud over the amphibian, hummed a brisk chorus of Amazing Grace and carried the intruder out to the two foot strip that is my garden. I released him. That is to say, I shook the napkin vigorously and ran back in the house, slamming the door behind me.

It's been said we live and learn. Venerable inspirational humorist Chris Clarke-Epstein says that each of us should keep a list of 100 things we want to learn. As goals are reached, you cross items off the list and add more. Not as easy as it sounds, but editing the list gives you something to do in the middle of the night when there's a frog on the floor and you can't sleep. It's not easy to think of 100 things you want to learn. I want to learn to speak Spanish; I want to learn to do the tango; I'd better learn more about frogs since we seem to live together. I'm coming to think everyone should learn to prepare a Crisis Kit for handling unexpected midnight emergencies. It would contain batteries for the smoke alarm, chocolate for strength, and a little plastic cup with a lid for catching frogs.

So the Great Frog Crisis is over. Everyone has their weak spots and we all have a lot to learn. But it's after 1 a.m. and I think the smoke alarm just went off.

I'm sure I turned the stove off, though. I'm not worried.

June 28, 2007

Recycling

There's only one thing wrong with my new recycling bin. Everything goes into the bin together, allowing me to feel virtuous and ecology-minded without the trouble of sorting and stacking. However, if something important is discarded by mistake, it's not easy to reach over the high sides to retrieve it. Unless you can reach in with chewing gum on the end of a stick, the only way I've found is to turn the bin over on its side and crawl in after the lost piece. Chances are that at least three of the neighbor's dogs and two squirrels will feel called upon to join you. It gets crowded in there. If it happens more than once, the neighbors will gather for the free entertainment and take bets on when you'll get out.

So I've decided it's really better not to throw anything away until it definitely won't be needed again. There's no telling when that might be. My inability to discard personal items, to let go of treasured mementoes or simple recyclables is legendary. I've been known to develop a deep emotional attachment to a matched set of cardboard egg cartons. Kenny Rogers may know when to hold 'em and when to fold 'em, but I just know how to hang on to 'em.

My purse, for instance, is sort of like Mary Poppins' carpetbag. It's battered and floppy from long use and filled with things that could have been recycled any time in the last millennium. It contains several small pieces of furniture as well as snacks for moments of low blood sugar. Of course, there's a pencil sharpener and pencils and an assortment of magic markers. A friend picked purse and contents up the other day. She dislocated her shoulder. "It's heavy," she gasped as she sped away to the ER. It's true that my purse weighs just about eight pounds, which is approximately the same size as a small dog or a large pot roast, but if I need anything I've got it at my fingertips. Of course, I won't be able to find it.

Then last Sunday at church, the sermon caught my attention with a message, which paraphrased a Boris Yschenko quote, "The trick to handling the past is knowing what to bring with you into the present and what to leave behind." Well, I thought, he can't be talking to me. I'm not leaving anything behind. I'm bringing it all with me. In my purse. Only the day before, the mail brought me an envelope from my sister-in-law, which she found among her mother's belongings. It was a letter I had written from Thailand nearly 40 years ago. In it, in the first days of our moving into our home in the golden Land of Smile, I described only the difficulty of settling in. My principal complaint centered on my inability to find disposable diapers for the baby and "being reduced to washing his diapers in the hotel bathtub." Obviously, instead of arriving open to a new experience in Bangkok, I'd stuffed all of the good old USA in my mental bags with me. I'd expected to find everything the same. I felt a certain exasperated pity for my 30-year-old self and threw the letter right into the recycling bin, but Sunday afternoon I had to go and retrieve it. I read the letter a time or two to remind myself that I don't need to keep carrying yesterday's limitations along with me. It's no trick to keep dragging the old baggage along, but going into the future it will be better to travel light. Arthritis will make it essential, anyway. I try to keep a positive attitude. "At least no one threw up on me," I reflect after a dull party—that kind of thing.

I'm coming to think positive attitudes are vastly overrated. I have a friend who has an unfailingly positive outlook. We all avoid her. But now, there is a new study saying that people who do not have a positive attitude can expect to live an average of seven or eight years less than those who are positive. My youngest son is a very positive fellow. Sitting around the table at dinner with him one night he announced, "Now we'll pray.

'God,' he began, "I want to thank you for the so-so day You gave me today."

So-so? Well, you can't snow God. He knows it was just so-so. We're supposed to get better as we get older. Oh, yes, I'm quite sure of that. Better every day. I've read that one thing that assures the next best thing to eternal youth is an attitude of learning. The trouble with lifelong learning is that the lessons are okay, but the exams are murder.

Writer-speaker Florence Littauer says, "I am enrolled in a crash course—life—from which I have no hope of graduating."

You have to decide for yourself what you want to bring along to the future and what you'll leave behind, but whatever you decide, I'd keep away from the recycling bin. And don't touch my purse.

August 24, 2005

Garage Sale

I just wanted to be able to put the car in the garage for the winter. This modest goal has been beyond my reach since about 1975, when the last square inch of floor, wall and rafter space was finally covered with cartons, bags and crates. Each was filled with personal items too precious to discard. So I followed expert advice and decided to "reclaim the hidden treasure in your garage or attic." I held a garage sale. It was the most demoralizing event of my adult life, if you don't count my 30th high school reunion.

The hard truth is that over the course of 60 years or so, you're bound to accumulate a lot of possessions. Accumulating is easy. Letting go turns out to be next to impossible. I've kept only the most valuable things. Each and every one represents a milestone of personal history. Beyond price are the 33 boxes containing homework of my children from preschool to college. I am saving their report cards for the entertaining day when I tell my grandchildren insightful stories about their parents' school days. Precious and permanent is the shoebox half-filled with the complete collection of all of their letters written home over the last 30 years. Then, there's the little box with all the kids' baby teeth, carefully wrapped in cotton. All right, I confess. I'm the Tooth Fairy.

Still, there is much that should sell easily. Each carton holds unique marvels that are bound to come in handy someday. There are assorted racks of clothes, all sizes and shapes, perhaps not at the height of fashion, but with lots of wear left. Many could be classified Vintage and Collectible. A prize example would be a perfect pair of hot pink stretch pants with the price tag still attached. I don't need them. After all, all of my pants are stretch pants. They have no choice.

You notice that I am still describing these treasures in the present tense. This is not an error of grammar. I still have every one of them. I held a garage sale, and I didn't sell a single thing.

With the help of my son who was evidently intrigued by the idea of actually viewing floor space not previously visible in his lifetime, I built shelves, counters and racks. A friend spent a week helping fix prices aimed at rapid removal. "Fifty cents, tops," became her rallying cry. When I closed the garage door on the night before the sale I no longer saw memorabilia, but potential income, perhaps even funding for a winter cruise. Even clearing the decks for the inevitable move to a smaller home.

Naturally it rained. It rains any day I schedule a garage sale. After the loveliest string of sunny days in Northwest history, it began to rain the minute my ad went online.

The sale was scheduled for 9:00, so prospective buyers arrived as expected at 6:00 a.m. In vain I pointed out the treasures—the manual ice cream freezer, lovingly turned by little hands on a succession of Independence Days; the plaster chef who laughed maniacally while dispensing a length of spaghetti-like string from between his puckered lips. Disgusting, but collectible. Ignored were the authentic imported drum tables, cunningly constructed from unused honey buckets, and the complete collection of *American Modeler* magazine, every issue back to 1953. The dust alone goes back to 1970. No sale.

I found myself slipping into the house to find something that someone would buy, just for the experience of making a sale. I sold most of the contents of the kitchen drawers including my ice cream scoop, melon baller and cherry pitter. I'll miss them. Do you know how hard it is to find a good cherry pitter these days?

When it was all over, I seemed to have slightly more than I had in the beginning, although that may be because everything was now out of the boxes and all over the floor. And I still couldn't get the car in the garage. Could this mean that my lovely treasures really are trash, after all?

A charitable organization which advertises pick-up service agreed to take it all away. The driver whistled in disbelief as he viewed the remains. "We can't take any of these things, Lady," he said. "We only take nearly new stuff. We don't do any mending or repair." Then he brightened. "But I could bring my own truck on Saturday and take it all away for, say, a hundred-fifty dollars." Clutching my treasures to my more than ample bosom, I showed him the door and started moving cartons.

It takes about two attempts to ease the car into the narrow avenue I've created between the old porch swing and complete sets of *Encyclopedia Britannica* and the *World Book*, circa 1953, but it's really not a tighter fit than the average parking garage space. When it's time to move to a smaller home, I'll be ready.

Autumn leaves are falling; Thanksgiving is on the way. It's time to count our blessings. Family. Chunky soup. Support hose. All the important things. I'm determined that I'll never have to plan a garage sale again. My treasures will stay my treasures. You can't put a price on memories, after all.

September 10, 2008

Downsizing

My grandson is scheduled to start kindergarten this fall. He's gone on strike. He's refusing to go because. Because a buddy told him you have to have lots of shots to start kindergarten. His conscientious mom has tried to convince him that all his shots are up-to-date and he won't need any more. But kids always listen to their friends, not their mom, and he just doesn't believe it. Change is hard to face at any age.

I know the little guy will come to love kindergarten, and I hope I'll come to love a pretty condominium exactly half the size of the house I have now. I hope so, because I bought it last week. I've been talking about a smaller, more convenient home for years and suddenly I've chosen one in a friendly, historic community nearby, where the main street looks like a movie set—sort of *High Noon* meets *Pleasantville.* I have about two weeks to get my house ready to go on the market. Can I do it? Oh, please!! Remember, I'm a motivational speaker. I spend my life showing people the way to do impossible things. I'm not sure about this, though. At least I won't need to have shots.

This change shouldn't be such a big deal. After all, 15 to 20 percent of the population moves every year. It's just that for the last 35 years, none of them have been me. I'm shaking in my shoes. "Are you really going to be able to downsize?" my neighbor asked. It all depends what you mean by "downsize." If you mean can I put six extra bags of odds and ends out for the charity collection, sure. If you mean can I get rid of half my earthly possessions by two weeks from Friday, I'm in big trouble.

Moving is never easy, though we moved 22 times during our army years. When we left Taiwan, a mover with a droll sense of humor carefully wrapped a tropic-size roach for us—the bug, not the smoking device. These hardy insects grow to about 5 inches in length. It was wrapped like a juice glass, and when I opened the wrappings the creature hopped down and ran away. It's probably still in the basement. Everything else is.

I asked my dynamic neighbor Gladys for advice. She's recently downsized into an apartment in her son's home. "Downsizing is very, very emotional," she confirmed. "It would help if you just walked out and let someone else do it." And that's possible.

Across the country, services are springing up that will take care of all the details. Some will even make a template of your furniture, working out how it fits in the new house. Then, they'll put everything in place for you, so you walk into your new home to find everything where it belongs—clothes in the closet and the beds made.

My realtor, who reminds me a lot of Mary Poppins with just a dash of Dr. Phil, suggests that I start by spending just two hours a day sorting and packing. Sure. At that rate, I'll be moved in 82 years. She tries to keep my spirits up with motivational affirmations like, "We'll eat this elephant a bite at a time." But that just makes me worry. She's probably seen an elephant down there somewhere.

I've mostly been taking things out of one box and carrying them across the house to another box. Then I write, "KEEP" in very big letters and put that carton out in the garage. Every box is full of memories. It's hard to know what to discard because even if I don't need it, I might have just what you need. For instance, what if you should need a ceramic cowboy that sings Red River Valley? What's the chance of having one of those in your own basement? Well, I have three. Their heads bobble. Mine too. At my new small home, a neighbor came out on his porch and watched as the realtor put up the "Sold" sign. "Huh. Sold one?" he asked her. "Are they Democrats?" Well, it all depends what you mean by "Democrat." I'll let you know.

August 31, 2006

Not for Sissies

I awaken every morning at 5:30 to the sound of vig-orously rushing water. Half-asleep, I try to imagine a waterfall, or visualize a splashing mountain stream, but no, what I hear is definitely flushing. I haven't yet met my upstairs neighbors, but I feel as if I know them well. Good to know external and internal plumbing is working well. I suppose the neighbors must be getting used to my routine too. We condo-dwellers learn a lot of unexpected details about each other.

The new home is just 1224 square feet from wall to wall, but it's all mine. Well, that's not exactly true. As any condominium owner understands, my new home is really only mine from the sheet rock in. The outside belongs to someone else. Still, it's a good feeling to look out the window and see someone mowing the lawn and someone else carrying away leaves and none of them are me. It surprised me at first when, walking out of my front door, I saw that it was raining cigarette stubs. This was unexpected. There they are, first thing every morning. It was a great mystery 'til the two young soldiers upstairs came, apologized profusely for the bad behavior of their guests and took them all away (the cigarette butts, not the bad guests). They haven't been back—cigarettes or guests.

I admit to shedding a tear or two upon leaving my good old house. The last weekend garage sale was very successful. It went much better after I started paying people to take things away. I wish I'd thought of that sooner.

Of course, I wasn't able to get rid of absolutely everything. The old garage is about half-empty, and the new garage is completely full of memorabilia I just couldn't part with. I don't know what most of them are, but I know I really need them. I still have one of the bobble-head cowboys, but the painted lady, all 6 x 8 feet of her, sold early.

Some things can't just be thrown away when you move. Not because you're attached to them, but because it's no longer possible simply to discard some items. Computers and copiers, for instance, must be safely disposed of or recycled. There's usually a charge for each computer and each monitor. It seems a cruel trick of fate that my reliable old Mac 512, a petite thing, incurred a double charge. I had to pay for both a computer and monitor on that one. Old copiers are recycled by the pound. My 1982 behemoth weighed 500 lbs. I should have left it where it was and turned it into a planter.

At least I can park the car inside at night. I just aim straight for the hot water heater and at the last moment make a sharp left turn toward the Christmas ornaments, and there I am, perfectly positioned. The tricky part is backing out without bringing any boxes with me.

Arranging the furniture in my new smaller rooms called for creativity. Dale and Scott, the affable movers, looked at the room arrangement with discriminating eyes. "You're not going to like the couch in the middle of the room," said Dale. "Put it under the window. You'll find it opens the room right up." As I set the dining room table straight across the room, Dale shook his head again. "Angle it just slightly," he suggested. "It gives a much more welcoming look." And it does. His partner Scott nodded. "Dale's gotten real good at this. You want to listen to him," he said admiringly.

Many of us residents are veterans of downsizing. Our informal support group meets around the mailboxes, where we talk about our lost, larger houses and the three-car garage that got away.

I haven't cooked a meal yet in my spotless new kitchen, and it's perfectly possible that I never will. I don't see how I can bear to get anything dirty. I have a large supply of paper plates, and so far I've eaten most everything cold. One of these days, soon, I suppose I'm going to have to turn on the oven and cook something. Not tonight, though.

I hear the rushing waters again. It must be 5:30. It's nice to know that everything is working and all is well with the world. I still haven't met the neighbors, but when we do finally meet, I won't have to ask how they are. I already know.

November 15, 2008

A Little Night Music

"What sort of noises?" the young man asked warily.

"Well, you know—noises," I said. "Nighttime noises."

His face took on a warm tomato hue as it dawned on him what I was talking about. I was feeling a little tomato-colored myself. I had never in my life expected to have a conversation like this.

I was very happy to see that this young soldier was safely home after more than a year in Iraq, but I had made up my mind that when he came back, I'd just have to speak to him before he took up his life in the condo above mine again. "You see," I said, choosing my words carefully, "my bedroom is right below yours, and I can hear EVERYTHING." "Everything?" he asked. I nodded mutely.

I thought I'd done my homework before downsizing to this perfect little condominium. I'd been sensible and systematic as I spent months drafting a list of all of the things my new home would have to have. I visited friends who had already made the big move until I found the floor plan I wanted. I checked out the Resident Owners Association to be sure I could live with the rules (no wind chimes, no garden, no bird feeder) and then I set out to check off the elements that would be really important to me. I had to see trees when I looked out my windows. Got it. Had to have a large, roomy kitchen. Got it. I wanted to feel as if I'd embarked on an adventure. Night sounds were not on the list. I absolutely failed to allow for the fact that I might be sharing the lives of the people upstairs—and that they'd be reenacting the beach scene out of "From Here To Eternity," every night. Theirs has definitely been more interesting than mine.

It has been half a century since I lived in a house with upstairs neighbors. In our early Army life at the Aberdeen Proving Ground in Maryland, my husband and I shared a duplex with another young couple. They came from Georgia. The wife's ancient mother (I suppose she was about the age I am now) stood on our shared porch and smoked her morning pipe while staring moodily into my kitchen window. I think I was sort of a reality show for her. At the Presidio of San Francisco I was awakened to the sound of an electric razor's buzz and the morning coffee perking upstairs. Here in Pleasantville, I am awakened at 5:30 by the sound of the dogs' legs hitting the floor. I'd say they have about 34 dogs up there, although the resident rules say there are really only two—but one is a Siberian husky. When the folks upstairs use the bathroom, the sound of flushing is like the rush of water through the Columbia River Gorge. Thank goodness they all sound healthy. The original owners of the upstairs unit were two young officers bound for deployment. In those months before they left, they somehow seemed bent on producing their own version of *From Here to Eternity*. Night after night. After night. After night. And I made up my mind, no matter how hard it might be, that when they came back, I'd have to speak up, and that's what brought us to this uncomfortable spot.

"Were you horrified?" he asked. I sighed and gave the speech I've given several times to my own boys. "No, Son," I said, "the act of love is beautiful. WITH the right person. And preferably after marriage," I concluded firmly. "It's just that I don't care to share the experience."

"You've lived a very full life," he said respectfully. Then he brightened. "Did it seem to you that it went on for a very long time?" he asked hopefully. I nodded gravely. "A very long time," I said. "I've always had a lot of natural stamina," he said happily, walking away with a bit of a swagger creeping into his step. Ben came back a little later to explain that he had miraculously found that right person to share his life and would be settling down in a larger home, many miles away. He had, he said, rented the unit above mine to a very nice family with a two-year-old child, an active two-year-old. As anyone with a toddler will tell you, all the parents—and downstairs dwellers—of that little person pray for is a good night's sleep. From my home, I enjoy the sound of busy, running feet all day long, but I'm happy to report that it's very, very peaceful at night. Sleep well, Little One. And quietly.

October 12, 2010

Warranty

"This product comes with a 15-year warranty," the garage door repairman told me as he clipped a crew cut of wires from the top of my new automatic door opener. "That means," he said gleefully, clearly expecting me to be thrilled, "that you'll never need another one."

I felt like a package of stale buns about to be pulled from the shelves. And the rest of me felt none too fresh, either.

"Young man," I said rather severely, "let me give you some helpful advice for dealing with your slightly more seasoned customers. My warranty may be going to expire on a certain date, but I don't plan to."

There seems to be a sort of reverse trend in customer service that imagines it's a selling point to be assured that your TV, garage door, car or joint replacement will outlive you. That might work when the customer is 30. It's not so good at 70.

I asked the wizard who performed my hip surgery when I might need a replacement for my newly installed plastic joint. "Plastic!" I exclaimed, deeply offended. It should have been titanium at least, in my view. "How long will that last?" "How old are you?" he asked. "You'll never need another one," he assured me.

It's not that I'm feeling persecuted. It happens to everyone. A friend and her husband decided to buy a car. "This will probably be the last car you ever buy," the salesman said earnestly. "So choose carefully."

As the years accumulate, it's impossible not to realize that other people's perception of me no longer matches my own. I see myself as youthful, focused, energetic—a twenty-five-year-old in orthopedic shoes, so to speak. The prevailing tone was set by a young grandchild, years ago, running into the bedroom while I was dressing with a horrified, "Oh, Grandma, how did you get all ruined like that?" and the terrible irony is that I was nowhere near as ruined then as I am now.

I can't deny there have been changes. In church last week, the worshiper sitting next to me at church stood up and struggled to raise the kneeler as if I weren't there, clinging to it like a plank on the verge of shipwreck. She tugged and wiggled it. It was sort of like being on the stuck end of a teeter-totter. "Wait just a darn minute," I finally exploded. This is not exactly the expected response to "Peace Be With You." Heads swung around in unison as if there were an aerobics class in session. It is true that I can't leap lithely to my feet anymore. I sort of struggle up, like an overloaded freight elevator, with several hitches on the ascent. When I reach the top, I stand still, looking around with what I hope is a pleasant expression while I wait for my knees to start working. Sometimes they do; sometimes they don't.

Preparing for a party last week, I shopped for beverages in the package store. The sign at the checkout stand proclaimed, "We ID everyone" and I dutifully got out my driver's license. I watched the clerk check three people in front of me, all in their 50s, but he rang up my purchase without a word. "You know," I said, "I would have felt better if you'd at least checked my identification." He gave me a long look and then said levelly, "Lady, sometimes it's best to let go of the dream."

There are still plenty of dreams left. I'm trying to learn serenity. It's not easy. Only this morning, our Tai Chi instructor leading the Yang Style Short Form exhorted our class to "Bring your hand out of that secret place." I'll try, but my mother used to get really upset about that.

I've been widowed for 30 years, practically a biblical number, but a date certain for my departure is still a most unwelcome idea. I believe you have to live as if your warranty would never expire. That's what I plan to do.

Up the road, Woodland Park Zoo in Seattle has opened their new exhibit of electronic dinosaurs that move, growl, and spit. I think I know just how they feel.

May 5, 2011

Tai Chi Chump

My black eye is nearly gone. It's not even what you could call black any more; it's more purple with a bit of yellow and rose, sort of like a Maui sunset. But I'm getting ahead of myself. I was going to tell you how it happened that I unexpectedly spent last Saturday evening in the emergency room and what I learned.

The day had started pleasantly. My sons visited and spent a happy afternoon throwing things away. Nothing seems to make them so happy as discarding my accumulated treasures and debris. They filled two big garbage cans and so were in a very good mood. I rewarded them with huge bowls of my Grandpa Franco's matchless Hunter's Stew. Even though I omitted the requisite squirrel and raccoon parts called for in the original heirloom family recipe, it was still very good with peppers hot enough to singe the hair off the back of the necks of diners and casual passersby alike. People who eat this stew regularly can go without constipation or haircuts for the rest of their natural lives, although it does tend to grow beards on ladies. And the dishes steam clean themselves. (Grandpa Franco's Hunter's

Stew recipe is reprinted at the end of this book.)

We were finishing off this memorable day with a brisk walk when, without warning, I suddenly fell flat on my face, knocking a flap of skin off my arm and blackening my eye. I don't know why. I didn't trip, but one minute I was up and the next I was down. My son settled me on a park bench while he ran to get the car and I sat with blood dripping from my fingertips, looking as if I were trying out for a very low-budget Halloween movie. I've decided that you should always carry a cell phone and a Kleenex when walking. Then you can call for help and mop up after yourself without wandering all over the neighborhood. Actually, I have a history of falls in unusual places. I've fallen going up stairs. I've fallen going down stairs. I've fallen just standing around. Once I fell into the dairy case at the supermarket, displacing several gallons of milk and completely demolishing 13 gallons of ice cream. I've accepted these unexpected spills as a fact of my life, and I never worried about it much, but now I'm taking it very, very seriously. As we get older and the bones grow steadily more brittle, we can't afford too many of these emergency room star turns.

What I learned from this experience is that I really don't want it to happen again. Ever. From now on, I'm moving my Tai Chi sessions to four times a week and adding sword form to the regular routine. That's bound to help, don't you think?

As we sat in the emergency room last Saturday, I fretted about the dismal turn of events. "It's all right, Mom," my son said, as we watched the doctor putting my skin back in place with surgical glue. "We'll just think of this as a bonding experience."

September 30, 2009

Uncle Ben Ate Hot Peppers

My Great Uncle Ben ate hot peppers at every meal, finishing with a pepper sandwich on the last day of his life, which came when he was 104 years old. He square danced three times a week until he was 101, when his leg was broken. An orderly dropped him out of his bed in the hospital. Even in his last days in a nursing home, his wheelchair was mobbed by flocks of ladies who pursued him from room to room like elderly groupies. He swore that his continuous diet of peppers was responsible for both his long life and his charm. I think it certainly had a lot to do with his alert expression.

Now, belatedly, medical science is catching up with Uncle Ben, crediting hot peppers with values from fighting cancer to extraordinary anti-inflammatory, analgesic and other heart-healthy effects. Never mind, we always knew that.

Family lore tells how my grandma's babies, when nursing, would gulp for cooling air between swallows of her very spicy milk, and then dive back for more. Seemed natural to us.

Carrying on the family tradition at the Naval

Academy, my Number Two son was challenged to a pepper-eating contest by an upstart plebe from El Paso. The entire brigade gathered to watch the competition, which was fought to a draw at 18 peppers each. I'm sure that all who hear the story will benefit from his lesson learned that, "they were hot going down and they were hot coming back up."

Every family has its comfort food. I know that there are whole clans out there whose family specialty is biscotti or Hot Dish with macaroni and cheese or some other dish that can't even stand up and walk on its own legs. In our family, though, the definitive staple is Hunter's Stew made with—what else—hot peppers. This dish was perfected by my grandfather, who allowed me to lead him about by the hand and to watch from a respectful distance while he created this masterpiece. The stew is traditionally made from parts of hapless game animals, hot peppers, and enough garlic to cause the stoutest germ and all but the most determined friends to flee. As my children grew up and prepared to marry, I always prepared Hunter's Stew for their rehearsal dinners. Best to let those prospective spouses know what they're in for right away, I say. But since I moved to my little condo here in the Enchanted Kingdom, I can only find three usable saucepans, so I've pretty much stopped cooking. Last week, though, a friend needed cheering, and nothing cheers like a big bowl of savory Hunter's Stew. I bravely got out my least warped kettle and prepared to work magic.

The process of preparing the peppers calls for almost surgical skill. Donning plastic gloves to keep the hot pepper stuff off my skin, I slipped the tray of peppers under the broiler 'til they were blackened and bubbly, and then popped them into a brown paper bag to cool. This sleight of hand causes the peel comes right off. The rest is easy. If you have moments of uncertainty, just add a touch of the wine to the stew (You know there's always a little wine around somewhere). After a mere 18 hours of cooking, it's as ready as it will ever be. The results are far from certain. When that same ex-Navy son came home last time, he dismissed the latest batch of Hunter's Stew as irredeemably wimpy. "It's supposed to be practically incendiary," he said.

Not everyone can eat hot foods, of course, but I'll tell you, there's nothing like seeing the sun come up when you've been awake all night after eating a hot pepper sandwich. It really keeps you going. Perhaps for 104 years.

August 15, 2010

Note: Just a couple of years ago I was introduced to that former Annapolis plebe who challenged my son to the pepper-eating contest. He is practically a folk hero in our family, so when Alvin Dickerson, formerly of the US Navy, who had become a minister, contacted me on Facebook, it was a wonderful experience. We often traded hot pepper stories. He called me Momma Red, because of the peppers. Sadly, we've lost Alvin to cancer, but he maintained his great spirit and sense of humor and was supported by his former classmates to the very end. In one of his last weeks, he sent me a gift of hot pepper jelly. I am still sorry he didn't get to taste Uncle Ben's Hunter's Stew.

August 21, 2014

To Thank My Teacher

An unexpected trip immersed me in the cold snow runoff waters at Paradise on Mt. Rainier. I lay there with the crystal clear and very cold water running into my undies, looking sort of like Glenn Close in the bathtub scene of "Fatal Attraction." It really was cold.

This was the first leg of a long-awaited trip with long-awaited guests from Taiwan. I was eager to show them my beautiful home state. This first stop in the incredibly crowded parking area was not promising. It was the closest we could get to Paradise. There was only a narrow uneven walking space between the road and the water. Anybody could fall there—but as nearly as I can tell, I was the only one who did.

Over the years I have developed a protocol for such occasions. It's amazing how often I've fallen full length into some foreign material. First, I lie still and keep my eyes shut tight. This, of course, renders me invisible. Everyone knows that. My theory is that when I open my eyes, everyone will have gone away, and I can get up and go on my way unobserved. I developed this procedure at the age of 12, when I fell in front of an oncoming bus, so it has nothing to do with advancing age. It didn't work then, either. On this lovely morning, just this side of Paradise, I finally opened my eyes to find four pairs of eyes watching me anxiously.

"Can you get up?" they asked. Well, I could. I just wasn't too sure I wanted to. On this carefully planned trip, I was supposed to be looking after them. Although we had not seen each other for 45 years, they immediately sized up the situation and decided that I was the one who needed looking after. So I climbed out of the water, and with towels stuffed into elastic and over various parts of my anatomy, we were off on our jaunt. We were five: Mr. Lee, our former English student, his lovely wife Alice, their daughter Vanessa and her husband Andrew. We were looking forward to a night at a beautiful country inn located in Ashford, WA. The inn advertises the chance to catch your dinner from the well-stocked trout pond. This was a big attraction the first night, but the fish poles supplied to us had apparently last been used around the turn of the 19th century. They were mended and patched, but Andrew had never before caught a trout, and he wanted to try. He cast neatly and the pole nicely separated into two sections, with one half collapsing in his hand and the other flying out over the water. Holding onto the line in both bare hands as if it were fishy dental floss, Andrew miraculously caught a trout. Any man who can catch a fish with a pole patched in the middle with aluminum foil is a gifted fisherman, no matter how well stocked the pond is. After looking at his catch for a horrified moment, Andrew said, "but this is a very good fish." He was proud to have caught it but he couldn't possibly eat it, he realized. He released the trout into the water. "Swim," he urged, making little patting motions above it. "It is not possible," said his father-in-law. "The fish is dead." Suddenly the fish splashed to life and swam far out of sight. Andrew breathed a huge sigh of relief and we went in to dinner. We were served anonymous trout caught by strangers., but Andrew ordered vegetarian lasagna.

Over dinner, I asked Mr. Lee the question I'd been dying to ask since I first met him. "Mr. Lee, how did you come to be our student?" As far as I could recall, he just arrived at our house in Taipei one evening, carrying sharpened pencils and a copy of *Meet The Browns* prepared to study English. Now he recounted the story of how he met my husband.

After World War II, Mr. Lee realized that there would be many chances for success for a young man in Taiwan who could speak English. Which he could not do. He had no money for a private teacher but he had an idea. Every day he would take the bus from the accounting office where he worked and go to the US Army Compound for his noontime walk. He would get off the bus, and walk briskly around the outside of the compound. When he saw an American soldier he would speak carefully one of the few English phrases he knew, "Hello. How are you?" My husband was the American who stopped to talk to him. Mr. Lee asked my husband to teach him English, and Roger said he really couldn't, "but my wife, who speaks perfect English, would be glad to do it," Mr. Lee remembered. "And of course, I was, though I was always puzzled about where he had come from." After we left the island, Kuney Lee continued to study English and sure enough, before too long that special opportunity came up for a young man who could speak English, and he got the job. Mr. Lee went on to retire as the Vice President of the second largest business in Taipei. "I came back to thank my teacher," he said simply. In the morning, before our drive to Northwest Trek and on to Chinook Pass, we visited the cemetery where Mr. Lee paused for a long silent moment at my husband's grave, placing flowers, then took off his hat and bowed three times, silently offering prayers or meditating, bowed again, now he was weeping, and then we all were as he silently said thanks to his teacher. So that's how Mr. Lee came to us, to say thank you to his old teacher and to open our eyes to the beauty of his culture and expand my heart. We learn from each other. It's time to thank my teacher. Thank you, Mr. Lee.

June 6, 2007

Monkey On My Back

My grandmother had a monkey on her back. She was small and brown and her name was Susie (the monkey, not my grandmother). My uncle brought the little creature home from the South Pacific as some sailors did who served in WWII. Susie slipped right into the rest of the menagerie on Grandma's Oregon ranch. This included a cowboy band and a black bear named Cindy. There were a lot of chickens, but I never got really close to them.

Susie's chief recreation was biting people. She didn't much care whom, but she seemed to think that I'd be especially toothsome. At six, I was small for my age, and she probably thought of me as a sort of hors d'oeuvre. We didn't get all upset about such things in those days. I just learned to keep out of her way. It was sort of like having a small annoying cousin. Swinging from Grandma's apron gave her a really long reach. I got very good at jumping sideways out of her way without even looking up from what I was doing. I can still do it if I have to. Our most lasting lessons aren't learned in school. Most life lessons turn out to be things you really didn't want to know. For instance, soon after my kids started school, I learned that children are hardly ever really sick when they: A) Get a tummy ache at school, causing the least convenient parent to be called to collect them immediately because they threw up, or B) The student gets a tummy ache at home that requires them to stay home from school, because they are going to throw up. Seriousness of the illness is easily determined by placing the sickie in a darkened room with no electronic companions. If they don't recover quickly, they really are ill. That's why they threw up. Otherwise, send them back to school. Repeat until a miraculous cure is achieved.

Many important lessons are learned from daily living.

For instance, a couple of weeks ago, my microwave died with a hideous shriek. During the prolonged wait for the repairman, I was forced to cook a real meal on the actual stove. While I was cooking, the phone rang. I did not want the grease to splatter on my lovely fake wood floor while I was talking, so I put my plastic cutting board next to the skillet to catch the splatters. That way I wouldn't have to turn off the burner. All who see the learning opportunity approaching raise your hands.

Right in the middle of the call, the learning

experience arrived. The cutting board melted and spilled carcinogenic rivulets of molten plastic into my dinner. At least I didn't set the house on fire. I waited until the plastic hardened and picked it out. There was still enough left for dinner.

When the repairman, Fred, came it only took him about 30 minutes to install a new microwave. I asked him my question of the day: "What are you learning right now?" At 50, Fred has a business degree and is working on his second career. He dreams of starting a business that will somehow help troubled teens. It will probably take some additional education. "Mostly all I know is what I don't know," he confessed, adding, "I wake up thinking, 'Please God, don't let me be out of time.'"

What happened to Susie? She lived a happy life, snacking on random visitors to Grandma's ranch, until she developed irreconcilable differences with Cindy the Black Bear. Susie bit Cindy. Cindy bit back. Goodbye Susie. Life lesson delivered and learned. All of this happened in rural Oregon in the 1940's, so there's no use yelling at me now. It's a jungle out there—and you can't monkey around. Turns out the learning really starts when school is over, and there's never enough time.

September 2, 2014

Superman Doesn't Live Here

I'm really disappointed in Superman. The action hero came to Earth from the planet Krypton when I was four years old. I felt we'd practically grown up together. But he let me down in my hour of need.

That hour came on a late Friday afternoon in spring of 1946, when the 7th grade children from my Bryant Elementary School class met with counterparts from St. Joseph's Parochial School for our weekly theological discussion and fistfight. We started by pelting each other with names that would certainly not be considered politically correct today. This quickly escalated to blows, bricks and garbage when available. Girls were main competitors until we reached junior high age. So I was lying there on the sidewalk with Timmy Groh's knee in my mouth, as was my Friday afternoon custom. Next to me, Pansy McCormic was beating Dick Stacy on the head with her world geography book. These were not years when you ran to your parents about trouble with other children. We were expected to work it out for ourselves, and we were expected not to get home too early, either. Luckily, we were all really inept. We tended to deliver blows to the forehead of our opponent with fist folded under as if tapping a melon for ripeness, so there was little permanent damage, but it did take a lot of the joy away from Fridays.

So while I was lying there trying to keep my front tooth from being dislodged by Timmy's knee, I remembered something important. In reading my favorite comic, I had noticed that Superman's great powers were conferred by his costume, because when he was dressed in his wimpy Clark Kent outfit he couldn't even peel a banana. In his Superman regalia, he was invincible. Based on this discovery, my contemporaries and I spent the week making ourselves Superman costumes from red and blue crepe paper. The next Friday, fully outfitted and making an unexpectedly attractive and visible target, we marched down Mallon Avenue to face our foes. They destroyed us even more quickly than usual. I had to accept the idea that clothes may make the man, but the costume doesn't make a Superman—or woman.

Even then I was a big proponent of avoiding the truth just as long as humanly possible, or slightly longer. While I was musing, we all graduated and went to different schools, and the Friday afternoon discussions faded. I went on fighting for truth and justice in my own inept way, battling unjust parking tickets, intransigent condo boards and other petty tyrants.

This year, the new Superman movie was released. It streaked in and out of theaters faster than a speeding bullet. "Superman is lost, angry, and frustrated," one critic complained. Heck. Who isn't? At 75, he's past due for his first midlife crisis (Superman, not the critic).

Last week business columnist Liz Zielinski wrote that our progress is sometimes stalled by our trying to continue doing what we think we're good at. She went on to say, "As the world changes around us our goal should become not to try to get back to who we were in the good old days, but to actually replace what we thought was a best practice with a better one." In other words, learn new skills for where we are now. I hate it when another writer makes so much sense.

It's been hard for me to face that I occasionally need some help keeping my balance when I walk. Last week my physical therapist decreed that I must keep a cane with me at all times. And use it. A cane!!

"I always have one with me," I said, virtuously.

"Try taking it out of the car," he replied.

So I sent away for a folding cane. It snaps to full length with a sound like d'Artagnan's sword and is covered with a gorgeous purple design. This is not a cane; it's a fashion accessory, which fits nicely in a slightly oversize purse. All of my purses are slightly oversized, so I've just reinvented myself. Your turn.

I never got around to seeing the Superman movie. He needs to grow up. I can tell you one thing: If Superman keeps trying to leap tall buildings at a single bound, he's going to need a hip replacement very soon.

July 1, 2013

The Brownies are Burning

I'm not sure how I managed to set the pan of brownies on fire. I didn't even know they could actually burst into flame. It's not as if I've never before burned any of my culinary creations. In fact, I have served so many charred entrees to gentlemen visitors to my home that it gives a whole new meaning to the term "carbon dating."

I am still shocked that the brownies caught fire. They burned with a nice, hot flame, which rose a good 10 inches without setting off the smoke alarm. I was able to put the conflagration out by smothering the fire with an empty dishpan while beating it with a spatula. It would probably have worked better if the dishpan wasn't plastic. Then I dropped the burned brownies, which tasted like the Wreck of the Hesperus looked, into the garbage and went out to sit on the porch swing and wait to see if the neighbors had called the fire department. They hadn't. Apparently the sounds and sights of crisis coming from my condo didn't seem particularly unusual.

Even the most incendiary cook has one specialty, and mine is my famous "Turtle Delight" brownies, so called because of a thick layer of caramel and pecans sandwiched between the layers of brownie. Naturally, when my son was coming to visit, I planned to prepare a big batch. The trouble is that the delicious caramel can turn to a glasslike substance, which sticks to the sides of the pan and the sides of casual passersby. It also sticks to any dogs, cats or raccoons that happen to be passing through. It often creates a barrier so impenetrable that it could be used as a garden paving stone. Sometimes it's necessary to cut away the whole outside caramelized frame to get to the nice gooey part in the middle. I reasoned that if I put a layer of baking parchment in the bottom of the pan, it might prevent the caramel from sticking. Incendiary cooks should not indulge in reasoning.

Sure enough, the brownies were perfect and tempting as they came from the oven. I set them on an unused burner to cool. They looked beautiful for the 10 minutes before they burst into flame. It turns out that caramel ignites easily, and apparently the fact that I inadvertently set the pan on a burner that was turned on high didn't help any. I had to serve my son oatmeal. Not oatmeal cookies. Just oatmeal. He didn't complain. He's used to these last-minute substitutions. I didn't tell him why. He didn't ask.

The worst of it was that the mini-conflagration burned the parchment paper into a thick charred circle of paper and brownie in the bottom of the pan. Nothing removes it, and that made it necessary to almost discard the beloved baking dish that has been my mainstay for more than 40 years. It was one of those white dishes with the blue flowers on it— dishes made from the same space-age material as rocket ship nose cones. These handy dishes could go from freezer to oven. You can't get them any-more—the dishes or the nose cones. You can find the dishes "showing some wear" online for about a hundred dollars. Or so. Like me, they're not getting any younger, or any cheaper.

I confess that I didn't actually throw the dish away. I put it in the garage next to the garbage can, but not actually in it.

You may have heard that I never throw anything away. That is simply not true. I throw lots of things away. Mostly apple peels. I only keep things that I am absolutely certain to use, like old peanut but-ter jars or empty toilet paper tubes. I have boxes of these obviously essential items. And then, of course, there are the treasures too precious to throw away, like handkerchiefs used for catching happy tears and that kind of thing. The dish might fall into both categories.

With Halloween coming, I might wrap up in my black State Fair sweatshirt and sit out in the porch swing to give brownies out to a few special Trick or Treaters. It's a good thing I didn't throw that baking dish away. I'm sure it still has a couple of good batches of brownies left in it. Maybe I could line the bottom with foil this time. I feel some happy tears coming on. Foil doesn't burn, does it?

Note: After this column appeared, one of my regular News Tribune readers went to the trouble of tracking down a dish for me that was like my last treasure. I am now fully stocked and when my brownies catch fire, I'll have to think of another excuse. Special thanks to Peggy Morris, intrepid baking dish shopper at Value Village.

October 1, 2009

Potato Beetles

In the spring of 1939, it was my job to pick the potato beetles and their offspring off of the potato plants in our garden. In the hot Montana spring the bugs quickly multiplied and would destroy the plants we needed for our main meals. My Dad's idea was that I should walk up and down between the rows, turning the leaves carefully to see that larvae weren't hiding underneath. Then, with one deft pinch I would pick up the bug and drop it in a coffee can full of kerosene, which would cause an immediate and humane demise of the wiggly critters. It was economical. You could discard the late bugs and use the kerosene again, if you caught any. Which I never did.

There were two flaws to the plan: I was terrified of the beetles and I was only five years old. They looked to me like ladybugs gone horribly wrong and wearing striped pajamas. When I managed to pick up a beetle, it made awful scrabbly motions between my fingers, signaling its general unwillingness to cooperate. I'd shriek and drop it on the ground, or my foot—anywhere but into the appointed receptacle.

I walked up and down the rows, clutching the coffee can, weeping and dropping beetles, which promptly scurried back onto the nearest potato plant.

After several traumatic but unproductive days, Dad offered a bribe. If I would collect a can of lifeless beetles, he would send away to the Montgomery Ward mail-order catalog to order the purse I was longing to have in time for Easter. I struggled, but the beetles kept climbing back over the sides of the can. Finally, my mother gave my father one of her patented Black Looks, and he sent for the purse. Right away. When the purse came, I was ecstatic. It was a lovely black patent leather with a silver chain for carrying and a Scotty dog with a red tongue printed on the side. It had just room to carry a stick of Wrigley's spearmint gum and a cotton handkerchief printed with violets. Somewhere in our great land people had begun using a new disposable product called Kleenex. In Warland, Montana, we'd have none of that foolishness. You used your sleeve for every day and carried a pretty handkerchief on special occasions. I also carried a penny for Sunday school in case the minister came. Church services were held in the same building that was the dance hall on Saturday night, and the minister, who sometimes doubled as the bartender, didn't always make it back for church. That was fine with me. The general store had great penny candy.

The beetles continued to munch on the potato plants, but it was my father's turn to dispatch them while he waited for my mother to stop giving him Black Looks and let him back in the house. I had a wonderful Easter. It's that season again. Priorities change with the passing years, but for me this is still the season of dreams, and anything is possible.

My neighbor has half a car in his driveway. It's not even the front half. It's all hollowed out. Just a shell, really. Maybe he's planning to make a planter out of it or a really big open-flame barbecue. He's doomed to disappointment, of course. Everybody knows you can't keep a hollow car half in your driveway when you live in a condominium. There's a whole book of rules and bylaws forbidding it. Still, man must reach for the stars, or in this case, the acetylene torch.

Daily we turn to the latest news to be horrified over and over by assaults and beheadings. It's important to realize that if we look around us, people are pushing through their fears and prejudices to try to make the world a better place. From St. John Bosco and St. Frances Cabrini churches in Lakewood, for instance, parishioners traveled to Haiti to do what they could and work with children in an orphanage. "We can help people," says Fr. Peter Mactutis, pastor of both churches. "It's important to step out of our comfort zone."

Many readers e-mailed that they're trying for five smiles from strangers after last month's column. Add just one step out of your comfort zone every day.

No potato beetles were harmed in the creation of this column.

March 30, 2015

Here's Looking At You!

My great-grandson is four years old. I have taught him many valuable lessons. I can't recall any of them just now. He has taught me how to watch him play games on my smartphone, how to stay out of range of his Nerf gun, and how to slide downstairs on my bottom. This last is a very valuable skill and is very much easier on the knees than the usual way. I am tempted to do it all the time, but his grandfather, who was once a four-year-old himself, now seems decidedly uneasy when I slide into the living room feet first. Some people just have trouble adjusting.

This holiday season has already required a lot of adjustment. Thanksgiving Day, spent feasting and trying to get in touch with my Inner Seahawk, was closely followed by the big winter storm in which a record-shattering quarter inch of snow fell on our community. It disrupted traffic and required our condo landscapers to blow snow off the leaves before they could pick them up.

The eye-opening event for me—notice the nice little play on words there—has been that I've had long-awaited laser surgery to remove cataracts from my eyes. The surgery went very well. I'm delighted to enjoy even the mundane daily miracle of being able to clearly see the pull date on the milk carton and the mold on the cottage cheese. Before this, I thought that green stuff was basil.

Every day is a revelation of seeing things I didn't know were there. I don't understand, though, why no one warned me that one thing I'd be able to see most clearly would be each and every one of my wrinkles. What once appeared to me as a few charming laugh lines now look like the end scene of *The Picture Of Dorian Gray*. "That's all right, Mom," my son soothed, "We could always see them. You're the only one who's surprised."

I should have been better prepared after I met an old friend at a party recently. He seemed to be crouched behind a potted palm. "I'm hiding from my wife," he said with refreshing frankness. "I just had cataract surgery," he explained, gloomily peering between the fronds of the palm. "Didn't it go well?" I asked, preparing to offer sympathy. "Oh, yes," he said. "My vision has been restored to 20-20. But now that I can see all of my friends, I'm in shock. You know, I thought we were holding up pretty well, but they're really old far—uh—old fellows, and my wife," he went on, dropping his voice slightly, "I had no idea she had so many wrinkles. I liked it better when I couldn't see them." His voice trailed off. "I suppose," he finished despondently, "it would have been better if I hadn't told her that." Probably. Apparently he hadn't yet looked in a mirror. Three million Americans undergo cataract surgery each year with a success rate of 98%. But there can be complications. "The piles of dust," one friend said promptly. "I thought the house looked quite respectable, but there are piles of dust and cobwebs everywhere."

My new, clearer vision brings some holiday surprises. It turns out that what I took for a large bruise on my grandson's arm is an elaborate tattoo. His little boys wrote their names on his arm, and he had the names tattooed along with their handprints. It's very sweet and touching, but I miss the days when we just hung the children's art on the refrigerator door and changed it occasionally.

As I wrestle with these changes, I've found myself remembering a poem I read long ago. I don't know the author, and the editorial staff at *Seventeen Magazine* where I first read it are trying to trace her for me. I'd like to find her because this poem changed the way I look at life.

This is what I remember:

"I will not be old even when I am bent and wrinkled

Where time has touched me.

When the first snowflake means only trouble,

And Christmas is just another day.

Then, I will be old."

It's never the number of days you've lived that matter or counting wrinkles or fretting over how things change. It's all how you look at it. If you're lucky, it's better every day.

December 29, 2014

Tai Chi Granny

The sword came in a very long box. As I took off the wrapping and lifted it out of the carton, I could imagine members of the ancient Chinese Imperial Guard in their padded uniforms, moving about with confident steps and menacing anyone in sight. I won't be doing that. I'm just trying to develop a little core strength and flexibility. I have begun studying the Tai Chi Sword Form. Very good for the elderly, one description says. My sword is made of wood. It has no sharp edges and that's a good thing.

My teacher, the Inscrutable Gary, is as always very patient and kind. To tell the truth, though, I think he may be a little apprehensive. He stays well out of my way when I swing my sword. But then, everyone else does that too. I have studied Tai Chi for five years, consistently displaying the same incredible aptitude I've shown in learning dancing, singing and playing chess. That is to say: Absolutely none. Still, everyone progresses, even me. I decided it was time to move to the next level. So I ordered the authentic sword from Amazon, where else? I am following the example of my mother, who believed that for a long, happy life it is important to learn something new every day. She took up pool. Not swimming, but playing. I ruled out roller-blading, and I can't get my leg over the Harley anymore, so it's got to be Tai Chi.

The starting position of the sword form is with the sword held in the left hand, facing front, the point just at the shoulder. Then with a clever twist of the wrist, which I haven't a prayer of ever accomplishing, the blade swishes around to the back. You see the problem. This was designed for men. If one has any protuberances on their front, they're in danger. Although time has stolen a great deal from me, it has left my protuberances intact, and I'd like to keep them. The publication of Harvard Medical School outlines the many benefits of Tai Chi (http://budurl.com/HarvardTaiChi), from reducing pain to easing a large number of physical problems and diseases. Because the muscles are relaxed, not tensed, it's suitable even for people recovering from surgery. It's also good for people who have previously shown no talent whatever for absolutely anything. I can do that.

After a practice session with my sword, during which I miraculously managed not to cut anything off of anyone, it seemed a good idea to blend a delicious healthy drink. So I unboxed the smoothie blender that's been sitting on my counter for a month. You can't rush good health. I used strawberries, bananas, added a few leaves of torn-up kale, an avocado, a bit of spinach. Now the interesting thing is that it's nowhere near as bad as you'd think. I made another one with only frozen raspberries and two leaves of kale and it was terrible. However, just as I was getting into the possible combinations, I read that too much kale can cause kidney stones and spinach can cause thyroid problems. I don't know whether to give up smoothies or stop reading.

For Mother's Day I was given a lovely pendant created by a brown bear at the Minnesota Zoo. My amazing daughter-in-law, who chose it for me, explained that exactly how the bear creates art is a closely guarded secret. I imagine the bear going into his cave, sitting down, adjusting his glasses and turning out a masterpiece with his plump little bear paws. His mother probably told him to keep moving and doing new things, too. Recently dark rumors have surfaced that the art is actually hijacked from work by the otters at the zoo. Presumably they can easily do the work with their little otter fingers.

I was outraged this morning to be awakened by the sound of someone banging on metal outside my door. "Neighbors!" I thought grimly, throwing open the door and getting ready to yell. It turned out to be a redheaded woodpecker, working on the metal No Parking sign by the mailbox. He totally ignored the wooden pole and tree trunks. What optimism! What confidence! I've been told it was probably a mating call. Louder is better, apparently, and you don't know until you try.

My grandson's coming to visit soon. We're all excited to share new adventures. He'll be able to recognize my car because I'm going to have one of those magnetic signs made. It will say, "Caution! Tai Chi Granny on Board."

It's nearly time for my sword practice. You may want to clear the area.

June 27, 2014

The Bibi Papers

Bibi, my geriatric Yorkie, has developed her own approach to crisis management. Whenever events become too taxing, which is about three times a day, she simply deposits a large and disdainful puddle on the shoes of the person who is causing her disharmony. I haven't tried that approach so far, though I have been tempted. Bibi seems to find it very effective. I will admit that I'm looking for some new techniques for handling stressful situations.

Good thing we have our animal friends to help us through difficult times. Sometimes, though, they just add to the problem. At my pet's last exam, for instance, the kindly animal doctor watched Bibi pace around the examining room.

"Look at that," he said accusingly. "She is so stressed. What have you done to her?"

Me? I feed this animal a specially designed diet and treat her arthritis with capsules, compounded at a "people" pharmacy. They cost about the same as a day cruise on Puget Sound. Bibi is 16 years old. Her groomer scolds me because I don't have my animal companion's hair clipped often enough.

"It's easy to remember," she (the groomer, not the dog) says in exasperation. "Just bring her in whenever you have your hair colored."

I don't really have my hair colored that often. It's just convenience that I carry drivers licenses with three different hair colors. You simply never know when you wake up in the morning where the day will take you.

I don't mean to whine, but life seems to be taking a complicated turn. I was away last week on business for three days and while I was gone, my house became haunted. Well, actually the house became weird. I have that from my on the spot expert. "The house is acting weird," said my daughter as I walked in the door. It seems that the burglar alarm now rings loudly at intervals, whether it is turned on or not and, worse yet, the television keeps turning on all by itself. I suppose this is due to some malfunction of a minute inner electronic chip—although that set is so old it probably still has tubes. For now, I'm leaving the TV unplugged most of the time.

So far, I'm not planning an exorcism, but I'm not sure it won't become necessary. In more orderly times, televisions did not misbehave in this way. My family had the very first television set on our block. Our Hoffman had a small round screen. It was sort of like watching a washing machine. This set was without electronic pretensions. It could be adjusted with a smart smack to the side with the Sears Catalog, or by moving the strips of aluminum foil hung from the rabbit ears, and it definitely stayed off when we turned it off.

I am ready to admit that I am tired of character-building opportunities to meet new challenges, but they keep coming. I'm spending three weeks in occupational therapy giving forced attention to a leg that no longer wishes to a team player. Lymphedema is the name of the problem, and I'm lucky to live in one of the rare American cities that has a clinic which deals with this condition. My therapist is smart, efficient, caring and very, very firm. Lots of relaxation breathing, she insists. Drink uncomfortable amounts of water and exercise briskly everyday. Get real. If God had wanted us to be able to touch our toes He would have put them on our knees where we could reach them.

My left leg is wrapped thigh high in elastic bandages, which means taking a shower with the leg in a garbage bag. When I do that, the bag slips. Then, I emerge with wet bandages hanging to all sides creating an uncanny likeness of Bride of the Mummy. Naturally, I am grateful to have this chance for self-improvement, but my inner self is getting water logged.

As the kids like to say, my plate is full. No more, please. I've already had a double helping of life and I'm passing on the next course. From now on, I'm simplifying everything. Hold the crisis. I've tried all of the tried and true stress management techniques, and done so much relaxation breathing that I sound like an audition tape for The Little Engine That Could.

I've been trying to remember people I've known who handled everyday crisis with grace and charm. My mother said to me once, "You only have to do three things to manage any situation—keep learning, keep dancing and do something for someone else every day."

At that time, Mom was 80 and bent almost double with osteoporosis. She still spent almost every evening delivering her universal cure of home-made chicken soup and Grammy Rolls to "the elderly."

But my favorite crisis management technique came from a friend who reports that she has this area of her life under control. When life gets out of hand, she goes to the Salvation Army thrift store (shopping is always good for stress), and there she buys nice, inexpensive dishes. She then takes them home and breaks them one at a time into a metal garbage can, enjoying the wonderful crashing noise as they hit bottom and she visualizes one more problem out of the way. Crash! Bang! Hmmm, that isn't bad. I feel better already. Say, hand me that platter, will you?

September 1, 1999

Goodnight, Bibi

She was a tiny brown and black fluff of fur when she came into our household. I never wanted a dog; I've never been an animal person. But the children were so lonely after their father's death and Patrick said the last time he asked for a puppy, all he got was a baby sister and they all begged until I finally gave in. Before that dog came in the door, on Gina's 8th birthday, I made the rules clear. They must take full responsibility. I would not touch so much as a can of dog food or a dish of fresh water.

Bibi set about training us immediately. Apparently sensing my attitude this small Yorkie set out to trash every item that belonged to me. Bibi could fly, or seemed to. She leaped across the tops of the furniture, her tiny feet a blur. She'd come to a stop on top of the big wing chair by the living room window to survey the view, barking her commentary on the world outside.

You wouldn't believe a creature that little could be so much work. There were constant messes for the kids to clean up. Let me tell you, I was glad she wasn't my dog.

Patrick explained that she didn't know she was a dog, anyway. She thought, he believed, that she was a short, hairy teenager. She deigned to learn only one trick, but it was versatile. It was masterminded by Patrick, who would point at her in the manner of a television evangelist and shout, "Repent." At this cue, Bibi would immediately raise herself on her haunches with her paws outstretched, as if in prayer. Irreverent, perhaps, but funny. The same trick also worked if Pat pointed an imaginary gun at her, and said, "Stick 'em up." She did the same hands up gesture and this time it was a holdup. Or if the cue was "Godzilla," she held the paws up and throatily growled "RRRR." Only a boor would point out that these were, in fact, all the same trick. Nor that the whole process bore more than a passing resemblance to that all time favorite, "sit up and beg."

Christopher at 16, not being an animal person either, planned to remain aloof but he recalls that he was soon won over by her wit, charm and warmth. Chris remembers the day a cat invaded Bibi's territory. The Dear Old Dog stood on the balcony, keeping very quiet, at least until the cat had gone, leaving some of its hair behind caught on a branch in the yard. Bibi did give the cat hair quite a talking to.

When the grandchildren visited Bibi avoided

trouble by walking away from toddlers whom he apparently saw as bald dogs of uncertain intention. Bibi wouldn't run away but would keep walking steadily, turning her head almost 360 degrees to cast worried glances over her shoulder. Of course, she was so shaggy, it wasn't always easy to tell what she was looking at.

One by one the children became adults and Bibi whimpered as they packed their bags and left for college, seeming to realize better than I that things would never be the same again.

I tried not to notice that Bibi was growing older and she courteously did the same for me. The high leaps were beyond her. She couldn't get to the top of the big chair any more.

Her hair turned to silver and so did mine. She accepted her locks with good grace and watched with bemused tolerance while I experimented with more hair colors than it took Norman Rockwell to paint the Four Freedoms.

And so it happened that on our very last night together, I gave her tiny sips of water from a medicine dropper while she licked my fingers, reassuring me with all of her great, faltering heart that all was well between us.

In the morning while her vet and I both choked

back tears, I wrapped Bibi in her old red sweater and held her tight until long after I was sure she was fast asleep.

And there, after all those years, it turned out that she really was mine after all.

August 30, 2000

The Last Reunion

This will be the last reunion. The postcard that came in the mail last week said so. "We don't have the time or energy to put these reunions together anymore. So the 60th reunion will be the last reunion for the graduating class of 1951-1952 from North Central High School in Spokane, Washington."

I'm not complaining. I certainly haven't been any help, and 60 years is a perfectly respectable number, though the best reunion I ever attended was the 70th reunion of Tacoma's Stadium High School. I was invited to act as emcee for the class of 1939, but those folks showed no sign of slowing down and they certainly didn't need an outsider to show them how to have fun.

This final reunion announcement expresses the hope that everyone will enjoy being together for one last time. The community has taken care to see that the occasion is not too stimulating. There will be no program except for an update from the current principal of the school, and the money left in the reunion fund will be donated to the college fund of the school. Perhaps everybody will sing "Red and

Black" one last time and festivities end at 4:00 in the afternoon in time to get us home for our necessary afternoon nap. Lest we be too sad, the committee comforts that they are available most Wednesdays at the tavern next door to the Spokane Club.

I continue to be proud of the fact that North Central has been one of the few high schools in the country able to keep their mascot, "the Indians." This was accomplished by inviting members of the local tribes (especially the Spokane and Coeur d'Alene Tribes) into the school to teach history, to supervise the way the tribes are depicted and to create historical displays together. So the students are having the positive experience of learning about local Native American culture in ways that wouldn't be possible otherwise and bring new meaning to a symbol that has come to matter a lot over the years.

Our 50th reunion was the most memorable. It was held the weekend of 9-11 while flights were still grounded, and our classmates got to the gathering any way they could. Everything seemed in sharp focus. As at all reunions, we checked for classmates with more droops or wrinkles than we had. Double points for finding anyone both droopier and wrinklier. I wore a red sequined dress so tight it made my support hose roll down around my knees. I couldn't walk because every step caused the hose to roll down further, but it didn't matter. I stood in one place and felt really queenly.

There are some reunions you wouldn't want to miss. This week both sides of my husband's family reunited to celebrate my sister-in-law's 85th birthday. There's always somebody who really stands out. Rock star of the event was baby Thomas, who came into this world with life hanging by a fragile string. Now, after many surgeries, he's an outgoing one-year-old with unstoppable curiosity about life. We watched him explore and finally escape the gathering through the back door. Never realizing he was under the watchful gaze of his mother, he battled his way through the yard and up the stairs to the front door. He wrenched it open and then stood weeping in stunned disbelief when he realized he'd done all that work just to get back to the same room full of dull adults he'd cleverly left behind only minutes before.

I've never liked class reunions. You never can find anyone you remember, and the jocks still won't talk to you. I've been very self-conscious lately about getting into large groups ever since that study was published that proved that older folks have a distinct "old people" smell. I explained to my great-grandsons that as you get older, your sense of smell becomes less acute.

"So I wouldn't know if I smelled," I said cheerfully, hoping for a disclaimer like, "You smell wonderful, Grandma." Their mom responded quickly, "Would you like us to tell you, Grandma Dorothy?" No, I wouldn't. There are some things you're better off not knowing, in my view.

Some family members met each other for the first time at our family reunion last week. My younger daughter stopped short when a cousin said, "Your dad was my favorite uncle. I adored him." My daughter shook her head. "I forget he wasn't just my dad. He was somebody's favorite uncle," she said wonderingly of the father who died when she was six years old. Reunions have their faults, but every once in awhile, you'll find someone who holds a bit of your forgotten history, and that can be exciting.

June 26, 2012

Porcupine Season

Did you realize that porcupine mating season is here? It lasts all the way until November. There will soon be a lot of little baby porcupines running around. Watch your ankles and don't say I didn't warn you. I learned this interesting fact the way I learn most interesting and reliable facts these days: From the Internet. If porcupines aren't relevant to your daily life, maybe you'll prefer this useful item from the Washington Department of Fish and Wildlife. It asks and answers the question, "How do you keep raccoons from getting into your garbage cans?" The answer is simple. You call out in a firm clear voice, "Raccoon, stop!" "This works much better than a scream, the report says." "Raccoon, go away," you may continue, speaking clearly and loudly. Apparently the raccoon will be so surprised that it will leave off whatever it is doing and slink away, embarrassed by having caused a problem. In extreme situations, you may use a broom to gently push the critter away. Wildlife is protected in our state, so we must proceed carefully. You don't find information like this just everywhere.

I just love the internet. I know a lot of folks who feel that since they've lived six or seven decades without going online, they can surely make it the rest of the way without hopping on, but they don't know what they're missing.

For instance, last Sunday our pastor told his flock that the average Mariner Fan spends up to 436 hours per season watching baseball on TV and the Internet. He issued a challenge that we should find an equal amount of time for prayer to balance that huge commitment of time for recreation. As Father told it, "A gentleman right there in the front spoke up. 'Father, that's just not fair. Mariners fans have to pray–a lot."

My Fantasy Football season isn't going at all well. For some reason Google has barred me from signing in, so my virtual team is playing without my expert guidance and I'm losing to absolutely everybody. That's all right; it saves me from the Grandma Guilt that comes with beating the grandkids and the great grandkids, which is the worst thing any grandma can do. The important thing is, we're all playing nicely together.

The pictures from my 61st high school reunion have been posted online. Our class photo is striking.

As in all of my previous class photos, I am nearly obscured by the classmate in front of me. That's good. That way, it matches all the yearbook pictures. Buried among the other shots is one picture of three semi-elderly women (my friends and I), who were six-year-old girls when they made friends across the garden fence in 1940. We keep in touch with e-mail and online. We couldn't do that without the internet.

Last Friday night, my youngest son posted on Facebook that my grandson (his dad calls him "Ichiro") was on his way to his first junior high school dance. You could almost hear virtual screen doors opening all over America as aunts and uncles and friends crowded in to watch for updates. "Sunrise, sunset," wrote his uncle from LA." "I believe he's too young and I would have kept him home," posted a neighbor. We all waited anxiously checking our Facebook entries, thousands of miles apart but somehow together.

Our baby is dancing?

Finally the report we'd been waiting for was posted by his mom.

"They had a barricade that halted the parents at the door," she mourned. "The boy said 'see ya' and took off into the darkened, thumping gym." A phone call to anxious Dad allowed her to "valiantly press on to the mall to stroll BY MYSELF with mocha in hand. Maybe this is not such a bad thing after all," she concluded.

A bit later, across America, virtual screen doors closed on the message. "He's home safe. All is well." You can learn a lot on the Internet. You just have to watch out for the porcupines.

October 2, 2012

The Vader Twins

When the rear-view mirror fell off of my car, I took it as a sign that I shouldn't look backward so much (and also perhaps that I should look around for another car), but when I turned on my computer this morning and learned that I had a message from Jesus waiting on Facebook, I didn't know what to think. I quickly reviewed my recent history, but except for failing to volunteer to prepare soup for the church supper, I could discover nothing good enough or bad enough to require such personal attention. "Jesus writes," the announcement began, "I've got to get an Amazon account." I'm familiar with celebrity endorsements, but this is ridiculous.

It turned out not to be THAT Jesus, which was a relief. It was a request by a gentleman named Jesus García for information about the best way of ordering a book written by a mutual friend. I don't know this Jesus. I barely know the mutual friend, but I don't dare quit Facebook. I'd never know what my kids are doing.

I decided to provide calming distance for myself by logging off from my computer and moving a few things around in the garage, which is what I do in times of dejection. The boxes make a nice noise when they hit the wall. There are many things from my parents' home I've never gotten through. This time I discovered a real treasure. Crumpled against the back of a drawer were two letters, apparently never mailed, which were written by my father nearly 18 years ago. One letter was for me and one was for my youngest son, his grandson, on the occasion of that young man's wedding.

My dad wrote of how this youngster, as a little boy, insisted on hearing only "polite and fair" versions of fairy tales. The Three Little Pigs must not be too scared and no houses could be blown down. Most of all, the Big Bad Wolf could not fall into scalding water. He backed into cold water and was so astonished he ran home to change clothes. Dad wrote, "We could not hurt big tough King Kong," who wasn't allowed to fall off the building "but had to climb down and swim home." I'd forgotten all that. But now, though my father's been gone from us for 14 years, I could see him sitting in his big leather chair making alarming animal sounds as the children climbed over him. You won't get that in an e-mail.

Dad was so ashamed of the fact that he had only a

fifth-grade education that he rarely wrote more than short notes. This message was important enough that he filled 15 tablet pages in labored block print.

It's true that no one writes letters anymore, but that's not a new complaint. My son, Dr. Chris, who loves and teaches Latin, proved it with this translation—from 110 AD, for goodness sake—when Pliny the Younger wrote to a dear friend.

"I am severely angry because for such a long time there've been no letters from you," he began. "I don't want to hear 'but I wasn't in Rome' or 'I was pretty busy' and may the gods certainly not allow 'I wasn't feeling too well.'" He ended with a request for very many very long letters. I wonder what Pliny would have made of Facebook.

This is a good day to write a letter to someone special. Even if they find it 20 years from now, the memories will flood their heart as the scent of wildflowers on the banks of the Kootenai River filled my memory when I read my dad's letter.

Memories are made every day. Last week my oldest son was playing Star Wars with his grandson—my first great-grandson. They had two Darth Vader action figures. One wore the iconic black helmet and accessories. The other was scarred, scuffed and had lost his helmet. Two Darth Vaders?

"Yes, "said the grandfather who was once my baby. "This is Darth Vader, and that one is his less successful twin brother, Darrell."

I could put that story in a letter—or post it on Facebook. Right now, I'm driving some soup over to the church supper. I'm taking no chances, and I'll be okay as long as I don't back up.

March 1, 2011

Laughter is the Best Medicine

Last Thursday, looking a bit lumpy in old sports clothes and dragging a wheeled mound of carry-on luggage behind me, I breezed through security at Seattle-Tacoma International Airport and boarded a plane for Salt Lake City. I always look a little strangely formed when I travel, since I learned that a sports bra doesn't set off the security alarms. It's true. No metal. My regular underpinning seems to be made of as much metal as a small munitions factory and always sets the alarms ringing and brings the security folks running. My travel life has been much more pleasant and much quieter since I learned this secret. I was on my way to the annual Conference of the Association of Applied and Therapeutic Humor in Austin, Texas. Well-regarded research suggests that therapeutic laughter is helpful for everything from lowering blood pressure to enhancing graceful aging. As a person who has spent her life raising six kids, I need to laugh a lot.

I had only a 45-minute window to make connections in Salt Lake City for my flight to the conference site, but our plane dallied on the runway. As departure time passed, the pilot's voice came from the intercom, "Folks, we're having a problem with our brakes, and we can't leave till we fix them." Everyone is in favor of brakes that work, but if they didn't get those brakes fixed in a hurry, I couldn't make my connection. Calling on the benefits of laughter, I stayed unruffled, even chuckled occasionally to give those little laughter-induced endorphins a chance to grow and develop. My seatmate looked distinctly uneasy.

After an hour, we were finally airborne, and the attendant served our nutritious complimentary snack of bagged pretzel fragments and a half can of soda. It took me only a minute to eat the snack and less than 30 seconds to spill the drink in my lap. My seatmate smiled sympathetically and passed me her napkin.

When the plane landed at Salt Lake City, I theoretically had time to make my connection, but as we sat on the runway a tantalizing distance from the gate, I knew it wasn't going to happen.

The pilot said, "They've sent us to a gate where there's already a plane boarding. We can't get in until that plane leaves." Turns out it's my plane. Who could be surprised? I sat with my face pressed to the glass and waved pathetically as it taxied past. Reaching into my library of laughter exercises, I breathed deeply and laughed aloud. My seatmate rang for the stewardess and asked for an aspirin.

Inside the airport, an agent in a red jacket gave me a ticket for my new flight—at 10 o'clock that night—and a voucher for lunch. Seven dollars. Knowing the benefits of a good attitude, I kept a smile on my face and my chins up as I trotted from one end of the airport to the other, dragging my mound of luggage behind me like the chains of Marley's Ghost. You'd think that with a little time on my hands, I'd have toured historic Salt Lake City, but airports haven't had luggage storage lockers since 9-11. So I walked, dragged, smiled and breathed deeply.

Still, I really lost only twelve 12, and I spent the next three days practicing laughter and learning. Latest University of Maryland studies show that laughter directly contributes to improvement of heart health and may even help prevent heart disease. I actually felt I had fewer wrinkles and more laugh lines as I climbed back into my lumpy travel clothes and boarded the plane for home.

From beneath the plane, as I settled in, came the unmistakable sound of—yes, it had to be—riveting.

"Folks," came the pilot's voice, "We're having a problem with the brakes, but if you'll just be patient. . ." I laughed out loud. My seatmate buzzed for the attendant and asked for a new seat.

June 4, 2005

An Unexpected Trip

I won't be traveling this Christmas. I took my trip for Thanksgiving.

It was going to be a Norman Rockwell-type feast with my oldest son and his family. The house was warm and inviting. I helped out by not making my signature stuffing, a step universally applauded. There were all the makings of a memorable holiday, so naturally I put my best foot forward. Then I caught the other foot and tripped.

In a move that would be hard to replicate in a *Dancing With The Stars* competition, I managed to fall against the dining room table, bounce effortlessly off the computer stand and land with my head more or less impaled on the decorative but sharp bottom rail of an accessory table. The next thing I knew I was lying on the floor surrounded by anxious family members I couldn't quite recognize. I didn't know who they were, but I didn't know who I was, either, so it was fair. They kept insisting it was Thanksgiving Day, but I had no memory of arriving for the festive meal, so I lay there trying to look nonchalant while dripping enough gore from a scalp wound to satisfy

Alfred Hitchcock and both Coen brothers. I could hear a young relative calling 911. "An elderly lady has fallen," he said. Well, that's a relief. He couldn't be talking about me. I didn't know who I was and I didn't know who they were. I didn't know what day it was. But I sure knew I'm not elderly. Or I wasn't when I got there.

The ambulance arrived with lights and siren blaring, which I'm sure the neighborhood appreciated very much. That's how I ended up spending Thanksgiving in the emergency room. They did not serve turkey, but I felt like one. And now I have seven staples in my head. This does not enable me to get radio broadcasts, as I had hoped. I suppose I must need an antenna of some sort. It does seem to have let in a little fresh air, though. Falls like mine have to be taken seriously. The Centers for Disease Control and Prevention in Atlanta says the death rates from falls among older men and women have risen sharply over the past decade. When you're past 75, as I suppose I must admit I am, you are four to five times more likely than those age 65 to 74 to be admitted to a long-term care facility for a year or longer after a fall. In other words, I was very, very lucky.

OK. I'll admit it scared me. I'm especially worried about the fact that many older people become so frightened after a fall that they severely limit their activity and soon become unable to be fully independent. We have to stay active to survive.

Take Santa Claus, for instance. We know the jolly old elf is, well, old and on the heavy side. He obviously doesn't eat right. Still, all that going up and down chimneys and jumping onto reindeer has apparently paid off. He goes everywhere he wants. Regular exercise is important, and the CDC says that Tai Chi is especially good.

So I'm off to my Tai Chi class this morning, wearing a fetching scarf, which makes me look alarmingly like my grandmother. This wouldn't be bad, except she's been dead for 50 years. It may not be truly fashionable, but it does cover the two-inch shaved spot on my scalp that looks sort of like pre-execution preparations. The staples are due to come out on Friday.

I'm determined to put on a happy face and look on the bright side. I'll be able to do it if I don't run out of under-eye concealer.

At the hospital on Thanksgiving, my son and I had a surprisingly good visit. We reminisced about other shared holidays and had just worked our way back to the year overseas when he dropped his brother in a benjo ditch when the word finally came that we could leave. "Good," he said. "We've about wrung all the joy we can out of the evening, anyway."

So here's to a happy holiday. May you wring all of the joy possible out of the season—but please don't forget, you'll enjoy it a lot more if you don't take any unexpected trips.

November 27, 2012

Not a Prayer

My prayer plant is not praying. According to the label, this plant takes its name from the fact that it folds and lifts its oblong leaves in changing light as if in worship. I was charmed by the idea and by the fact that it's supposed to be easy to care for. So far there's no sign of folding, lifting or praying, and I'm beginning to be afraid that my plant may be an atheist.

We all have our gifts, and mine is the uncanny ability to kill every plant I touch. For a while, I took the easy route and replaced all of my living plants with plastic ones, which I thought would be indestructible. I put plastic plants along the top of my kitchen cabinets with the idea that they'd brighten the place without requiring cleaning. I suppose after six years they may have gotten a little dusty. It turns out the dust is all that was holding my ivy together. Over the course of time, the ivy leaves have wilted away. Nothing left but stems. I didn't know that could happen.

Usually plastic foliage can wait, and usually I

wouldn't even start thinking of plants until spring but something unexpected happened. A week ago, in the dead of winter, I suddenly had a plant crisis.

Last spring Number Two Son (The number refers to birth order, not character evaluation) sent me a gorgeous basket of plants. I can't imagine what he was thinking. I was so touched that, incredibly, I managed to keep it alive for six whole months, a new record. Then came that heavy freeze in January. I left the basket outside one night too long and everything froze.

I'm very reluctant to bring outside plants into the house because of the little green tree frogs, which live on my porch. They move into the planters to get out of the cold. When they're brought in the house and warm up, the frogs hop out for convenient if unintended squashing. I stepped on one in the middle of the night a couple of years ago. It was not a happy experience for either of us. So I've developed a Frog Early Warning System (patent pending) to notify the little fellows when a move is immanent. My method is to leave the planter on the porch by the door, and every little while I go out and hit the container smartly with a broom handle.

The resultant noise and vibration serve as my eviction notice to possible tenants. When I'm sure they're all out—an inexact science at best—the planter can come in. There are those among you who will protest that this is upsetting to the frogs, but so is being stepped on. While I was evicting the frogs, that heavy frost came along and the plants were beyond rescue. I checked at the Home and Garden Show for something sturdy. They offered me a grey fuzzy nubby cactus, which had the advantage of looking as if it were already dead, saving one whole step.

I should be able to raise thriving plants. More than 29 million American households have container gardens. My daughter raised a whole vegetable garden last year on a porch smaller than mine, and my dad grew his beloved tomatoes in a small, raised bed long after his knees refused to allow him to get down to their level.

I settled on six plants whose labels proclaimed them "easy to raise." They practically shrieked and reached back with their little tendrils to their companions as I took them away. Besides the sturdy plants, I chose one irresistible beauty from the tropics called China Doll. It's delicate and probably won't make it through the night, but it was still alive 12 minutes ago.

I've put the basket back together, and if you don't tell my son, he probably won't notice that I killed his original gift.

There's still no sign of supplication from the prayer plant, but I think I know what the problem is. It has probably sensed that from the moment it came to my house, it didn't have a prayer.

January 29, 2013

My Father Told Me

My father believed in happy endings. So he read books backwards—or at least he started at the end. He would select one of his beloved western novels, Louis L'Amour or Zane Grey, where of course, the women were virtuous and the good guys wore white hats. Then he would open the book and read the last page. Only when he was sure the same people appeared on the first page and the last would he invest his valuable time in reading the book.

Dad wore a white Stetson hat all his life, and from him I learned to identify good books and good guys. My father was a giant. At least that's how he looked to my four-year-old eyes. Dad worked in the section gang laying the Great Northern railroad tracks that ran along the shores of the great Kootenai River and on past the metropolises of Libby (Pop. 1837) and Jennings (Pop. missing according to 1940 census). It seemed to me he had to stoop to keep his red hair from brushing the ceiling of the tarpaper shack we rented from the railroad. I thought he was bent with the wisdom of being ancient. He was twenty-eight years old at the time. He had never gone beyond fifth grade.

I feared my father as I feared God—more, really. God seemed distant, but my dad was there every day, sternly outlining chores to be done and accepting no excuses. And yet, he went about singing in his considerable voice. "Climb Upon My Knee, Sonny Boy," he would bellow at the top of his lungs, and "My Wild Irish Rose" and "California Here I Come." What he lacked in tunefulness he supplied in volume, and I learned that making a joyful noise can be more important than making a tuneful one and that you'd just as well make the best of things.

My father ran away from home to join the Marines when he was 14, and finished boot camp before his parents searched him out and took him home. He was sternly watchful of me in my growing up years and suspicious of any young man who offered attention. "They're only after one thing," he would say, darkly; "I am a man. I know," unconsciously insulting himself. I had no idea what that one thing was then, and I'm none too sure now. My potential suitors would ask in a fearful voice, "Is Mr. Conway home?" If he was, they were pretty likely to disappear and never come back.

Yet he gave good advice. Showing off my engagement ring, I asked, "What's the best way to take care of the diamond?" Nobody I ever knew had a diamond. Mine was tiny, but it was still quite thrilling.

"I think you're supposed to soak it in dish water three times a day," he said.

He didn't quite trust the young soldier who had given me the ring, and he never stopped being angry when our military assignments took us far away.

Then suddenly, by some alchemy never fully explained, the redheaded giant turned into someone called "Grandpappy" who frolicked and rolled on the floor with his grandchildren. He told them uproarious stories that gave fresh motives and aspirations to characters like the Three Little Pigs who, it turned out, were not underachievers but merely possessed of an inadequate skill set. I rejoiced in getting to know my parents as fellow adults and grieved for my own children because their father died before they could enjoy that metamorphosis.

Yesterday I came back from visiting my youngest son in Minnesota, where I watched bemused as, wearing his beloved Mariners jersey, this young father unflappably doled out kisses for "owies" and changed poopy diapers for his two young sons while cooking dinner for the family (Yes, of course he

2

washed his hands in between. What do you think?).

So I want to raise a slightly late, slightly out-of-tune hymn of praise in honor of the fathers who are at this moment changing diapers, coaching Little League, or keeping vigil over a sick child. And I'd like to offer a whole bouquet of roses in memory of my Dad, the man who taught me to tell the good guys from the bad guys and to go straight to the happy ending.

September 4, 2009

The Cowboy Goes Home

My father always said that he could tell when he'd first met someone by the name they called him. Over the course of almost 90 years, he'd met a lot of folks. And he'd answered to half a dozen names.

He was Joe when he grew up in a West Virginia mining town, Red in the oil fields of Oklahoma and Buck as a cowhand in Texas. The name settled into a whimsical "Grandpappy" when the grandchildren came (my mother was Grammy), and in the last years, with a host of health care workers, he was just plain Joe again.

To his best friend, Bill, Dad was always The Cowboy. "How's The Cowboy?" he'd ask when he made his daily visit. Dad loved to talk abut his days on the range in the choking dust of the Texas plains. The sun was so intense, he declared with a straight face, that the lizards carried sticks in their mouths. They'd spear the sticks into the sand and perch on them when the scorching Texas heat got to be too much for their little lizard feet. Most of all, Dad loved to tell about the years of the Great Depression when he and my mother were newlyweds. She kept his spirits up when he couldn't find work, singing and pasting strips of newspaper to the walls of their tarpaper shack to make it pretty and to keep the cold wind out.

"Never a word of complaint," he'd say, shaking his head in wonder. "I could never do enough to make up to her for that."

That never changed. Even in the last months of her life, he'd watch her moving slowly on her walker, and I'd hear him say under his breath, "Damn! I like that girl!" Listening, I understood that she was still 16 years old for him, even after 63 years of marriage. He was stunned to have outlived my mother. That was never in the plans. He could not fathom how she could be gone, but he was determined that he'd manage alone. Bill's wife had died years before. He and Bill would look after each other.

For about six months, they managed. Then he called me one night and said, "Honey, I can't find Mother. Do you know where she is?"

That was the beginning of a fruitless tour of doctors' offices, always ending with the same diagnosis. Dementia, they said, not Alzheimer's, but not reversible, either. Dad became convinced that Mother was out shopping. Knowing Mom, this was a fairly credible idea. He believed he had to be home when she came back, as she surely would do. That settled it for me. I would keep him home, no matter what.

There are many challenges unique to being a long-distance caregiver. Like many members of the "Sandwich Generation," I now had to keep my home and business going in Tacoma while looking after Dad in Spokane. Although he required a caregiver 24 hours a day, Dad was not eligible for help from most agencies. With the help of his very caring physician, we put together a health care team. To me, this team approach is vital for successful long-distance care. In addition to his doctor, our team included a private nurse manager who visited him at home three times a week and phoned daily. A bath aide from Family Home Care came twice a week, and he was eligible for help with that expense. Finally, after a long frustrating search, we found a wonderful, caring woman to take care of him, and our team was complete.

This may seem like a lot of folks to care for just one gentleman, but the mutual support and objective reports of these people assured me that Dad was getting the best care possible, even though I was miles away. Ultimately, we were able to bring the cost per month to less than a nursing home would be.

Of course, there were crises, like the time Dad called the fire department, "to see how fast they'd come in case of an emergency. And," he said with satisfaction, "they came really fast." Still, our team kept him home happy and, until the very last days, in excellent health.

Inevitably the day came when, sitting in the Intensive Care Unit at a hospital in Spokane, I held my Dad's hand while he finished his journey. Afterward, the nurse and I bathed him and slipped him into a clean nightgown for his long rest. I said good night and realized that after years of caring for my mother, my aunt and my dad, I had just become the oldest living member of my family.

To whom will I turn for wise advice? Dad would have consoled me with one of his endless resources of pithy quotes attributed to a dubious source. "This, too, shall pass," he would inform me solemnly. "Abraham Lincoln said that," he'd add. He gave Honest Abe credit for most of his quotations. Good advice, though, and the best I can get right now. The Sandwich Generation days are behind me: The Cowboy has gone home.

June 6, 1997

End of the Sandwich Generation

Today is my last day as a member of the Sandwich Generation. That term, of course, refers to those who are caught between caring for parents on one side and for raising children on the other. This results in the feeling of being the filling in a sandwich that everyone wants to bite but no one finds flavorful. Many days in recent years I've felt like the bologna stuck in the middle—and a little green around the edges at that. There is no membership card showing status in the Sandwich Generation, but if you are a member you know it. You've paid your dues in 2:00 a.m. phone calls and hours spent making doctors' appointments and giving long-distance care.

After today it's all over for me, and I have to admit it feels a little strange. Naturally, such landmark events don't happen all at once. This one began six months ago. It was a baking hot day when I stepped out of the August sun and into my parents' house for the last time. Every room was filled with small tables. In the kitchen, where my mother cooked so many spaghetti dinners and baked delectable chocolate chip cookies, there was small bric-a-brac marked $1 each.

There were silver spoons engraved with the name of the old Spokane Hotel—$8 each. Casey, the estate sale lady, raised an eyebrow at these—but it was okay. Employees were entitled to buy the silver when the hotel changed silver patterns. "They're paid for," I grinned. It's all paid for. I couldn't resist picking up one thing after another 'til my arms were filled. Casey followed me about good-naturedly. "Don't forget," she said, "if you take too much away, it won't be a good sale." Still, it's as if you could know there was going to be a fire or a flood and you could choose what to save.

I saved the porch swing. All of the grandchildren and great-grandchildren rocked in it with Grammy and Grandpappy on countless summer nights. It had to come away with me. We rescued all of the personal pictures, including the one of stern-faced Great-Grandmother Caroline. She had every reason to be grim. She was the mother of 24 children. Here was a lady who was both Roman Catholic and profoundly puzzled. She lived to be very old, but she didn't smile much. Among some rolled-up fabric remnants, we found a real treasure. It was a needlework sampler worked in red thread on coarse linen. Great-Grandma Caroline stitched it almost 100 years ago. When on earth did she find time?

We brought away every scrap of paper with personal writing on it, like my Dad's draft notice from World War II. "To all who read these presents, Greeting," it began. There were other treasures. My 8th-grade diary. What a dull little girl I was. My high school annual. What a plain teenager I was.

There was my official engagement photo showing my husband-to-be and me posed before the photographer's weary rattan screen. The portrait is retouched so much that we look like burn victims with the skin just growing back. That look was popular in engagement photos in the '50s. Don't know why. We put that picture, too, into the boxes and carried them out.

There were hundreds of people at the sale. They began to gather on the sidewalk in front of the house early in the morning to be admitted in groups of 20 for security's sake. I understand that the green glassware sold quickly. So did my Dad's motorized reclining chair. Afterwards, St. Vincent DePaul came to haul away the leftovers; a crew cleaned to the walls, and on the 15th of the month the new people moved in. They are a nice young couple. I had hoped for someone who would love the house and I think they will. Then I was on my way out. I stopped for a moment in front of the house to look at the spot where my mother planted dusty-looking purple-white flags that first grew near my playhouse during my Montana childhood.

My son and I climbed into the U-Haul truck and drove away without looking back. I thought that somewhere along the line, I'd take a few minutes to cry just a bit, but somehow the right time never came.

Now I'm addressing and stamping the last letter to the attorney, and the Estate of Joseph L. Conway is settled. It's official. I am no longer a member of the sandwich generation—Sandwich Generation—or at least, I'm not in the middle anymore. The kids will take over that spot. I'll have to start being very nice to them, won't I?

I'll send them special valentines this year. I'm going to write each of them a letter and tuck in a memento from their grandparents' home. Then I think I'll see if I can get Stephen to come and put the hooks under my deck for the old green swing. Even though it's a little cold, I'll sit out there and swing. Maybe I'll finally have my little cry. And that's no bologna.

Note: I drove by my parents' house just one more time, a couple of years ago. All of the flowers, the flags from my playhouse and roses my parents had loved so much had been removed, and the house looks sad and a little run-down.

It's true, isn't it? You can't go home again. You have to carry it in your heart. At least the old swing is on my front porch. I sit in it most every day. It closes the circle in a way.

August 4, 1997

Grandpa Franco's Hunter's Stew

Of course, Grandpa never wrote down his recipe. I have the original copy of this facsimile in my mother's handwriting. Of course, she never wrote down recipes, either. So it's her approximation of his facsimile, but this will get you started until you're ready to make up your own.

Peppers and Vegetables:
About eight peppers of different sizes, colors and degrees of heat.
one head of garlic
one or two onions
one 15-oz. can diced tomatoes
one 15-oz. can stewed tomatoes
Approximately one cup red wine (optional—Mom never used it. I always do.)

Meat:
one lb. each of chicken with skin and bones, beef round steak, pork roast, and boiling beef with bones. If you have a squirrel, you should throw it in, too.

A bit of venison would be good. Whatever you have... I always do).

Procedure:

1) *Select peppers*—about two each nice green, red and yellow sweet peppers. For hot peppers, it's best to start light, unless you really know the palate of your diners. I'd say start with two or three nicely shaped Hungarian wax peppers.

2) *Select meat*—Remember that the original stew had several different kinds of game, so get at least three different kinds of meat—pork, round steak and chicken, for instance—and definitely soup meat with bones. The bones and chicken skin will give flavor. It really needs beef.

Cube the meat.

3) Always wear gloves when working with peppers. Wash and place on a tray under the broiler until they are blackened and bubbly. Personally, I don't peel the sweet peppers, but that's up to you. When the peppers have bubbled, slide them into a brown paper bag, close it tightly and set them aside for about 20 minutes. While they cool, you can put your meat under the broiler to brown. Take care to

keep the peppers off your skin. If you do burn your skin, rub it with olive oil or bathe the afflicted spot in milk.

4) Put then put a sturdy Dutch oven on a medium hot burner and sauté three cloves of garlic with one chopped-up onion. Dice sweet peppers and add them to the pan. While they sauté, put the gloves back on and take the peppers out of the bag. They should slip right out of their skins under running water. Slit the peppers. Remove all seeds and white ribs from inside of the peppers, dice all the peppers, and put them into the pan. Sauté together, then add the meat. Take off and discard the gloves. Add one 15-ounce can of stewed tomatoes and one 15-ounce can of diced tomatoes.

Sauté peppers and veggies together, then add the meat. Add one 15-ounce can of stewed tomatoes and one 15-ounce can of diced tomatoes.

Add 1/2 tsp oregano.
1/2 tsp salt (or to taste).
Red wine to taste.

5) When the stew comes to a boil, turn it down to simmer and let it cook at least six to eight hours.

You can eat it sooner, but it won't be the same. Overnight is even better. Personally, I don't like a crock-pot for this, but it will work.

6) Add a half-cup of wine every two hours or so. If it becomes too thin for your taste, you can reduce the mixture by turning up the heat. You can also thicken it by adding tomato paste, but I prefer not to. If you add the paste too late in the process, you'll be able to taste it.

Serve in bowls with fresh hard rolls. It has become more difficult over the years to suit everybody's taste. Most of my Hunter's Stew addicts can't eat hot pepper any more. I've tried the compromise of cooking a mild stew with additional hot peppers to be added, but that really doesn't work. The only thing to do is to make two or even three grades of stew like in Thai restaurants. But at least, you can start off this way.

An Amazing Day

"Have an Amazing Day!" the clerk chirped as I left the store. That strikes me as a terrible idea. There comes a point in life where, you can only handle so many amazing days. I mean, most of my days are amazing anyway. If I can find my glasses, that's amazing. If I back the car out and remember to raise the garage door, that's amazing. Do me a favor and don't wish me too much amazement.

But what I have found out is that even the least amazing days can be filled with excitement and joy. So that's what I wish you'll find as you read this book. That life can be better every day.

Have an amazing day, now!

The Facts of Life

The facts of life came in the mail in a plain envelope. It was brave of my mother to send for the book it contained, which was called *Where Do Babies Come From?* The magazine ad promised it would explain the beginnings of life in a clear, easy to understand way that mothers and daughters could share. That kind of sharing was very rare in 1946 when interesting things still came in the mail.

The first page began, "I am an adolescent girl." Of course a man wrote it. Never mind. I was twelve and desperate for information. Explicit scenes in movies consisted of couples sharing intense, slightly constipated looks, mysteriously followed by pictures of fireworks exploding, even if it wasn't the 4th of July. In short, I didn't have a clue.

Mom and I read the book together. There was a guest appearance by the birds and bees. Then it got down to business. The most startling bit of information was the sinus-clearing announcement that how "the male plants the seed (from which a baby develops) is by use of a tube which he carries." Well, this was news! I visualized something like a soda straw or a pea shooter made of that new fangled plastic stuff that was beginning to appear in stores, possibly decorated with stars and stripes, or something celebratory. I imagined that all the truly hep (hep is right. The word didn't become "hip" for almost a generation.) fellows, who were really in the know, would probably have such an object in their rear pocket at all times, just in case. Whenever I saw a male person, I'd maneuver a look at his rear pocket but I never managed to glimpse the gadget.

When we finished the book, Mom cautioned me not to share this newfound information with any of my friends. Mothers preferred to tell their daughters at just the right time, which was usually never, she explained. Of course, I said. I understood, I said. What I understood was that nobody was going to beat me in passing this choice intelligence on. I might never have such a scoop again in my life. Sure enough, I never did.

I went right out, gathered up my friends and taught my first seminar in the parking lot of the Grace Baptist Church. I only charged my audience 10 cents and half a banana Popsicle apiece. It was a bargain. I'm pretty sure that if I could have got hold of those soda straw things I could have charged 50 cents.

It is difficult now to imagine the climate of thos. days after the war. We had spent years collecting newspapers, doing without shoes and meat, rolling gum wrappers into balls of tin foil. and being assured, by authorities as credible as Mickey Mouse and Donald Duck of our ability to act wisely in all situations and of our superiority over people who were different than we were.

There was someone else in my life in those days who bravely shared a truth that I would carry all my life. That was my Sunday school teacher. Mr. Randall loved America and he loved us. It bothered him to see old prejudices reappearing in our lives.

One Sunday, he brought a black envelope and a white envelope to class and held them up for us to see. What were they? Envelopes, we agreed. Next, he brought out a silver dollar. We were electrified. Children of what would today be called the working poor, we could have done a lot with that dollar. He slipped the silver into the white envelope. What is it now? A silver dollar in a white envelope! Can you spend it? Do you want it? Yes!

Next, he slipped the dollar into the black envelope. Has the value changed? Can you spend it? Do you want it? Yes! Oh, yes!

"For the rest of your life, when you meet someone

neone" he said, "Never look at the color
lope. Look at what's inside." Then he
me the envelope with the dollar. I was always
teacher's pet. But somehow I understood that this
one wasn't mine to keep, but to pass on and I'm
passing it on to you today.

Sometimes, the most important facts of life can
come in a plain envelope.

Dorothy Wilhelm still gives seminars. She is a
professional humorist and speaker. Reach her at
PO Box 881, DuPont, WA 98327, e-mail Dorothy@
itsnevertoolate.com, phone 1- 800-548-9264

July 1, 2015

Dorothy Wilhelm
P.O. Box 881
DuPont, WA 98327

www.itsnevertoolate.com
Dorothy@itsnevertoolate.com

163

9 780692 397404